AMY TAN

ASIAN AMERICANS
OF ACHIEVEMENT

ASIAN AMERICANS
OF ACHIEVEMENT

AMY TAN

SUSAN MUADDI DARRAJ

CHELSEA HOUSE
PUBLISHERS
An imprint of Infobase Publishing

YJ
92
Tan

Amy Tan

Chelsea House
An imprint of Infobase Publishing
132 West 31st Street
New York, NY 10001

ISBN-10: 0-7910-9269-0
ISBN-13: 978-0-7910-9269-9

Library of Congress Cataloging-in-Publication Data
Darraj, Susan Muaddi.
  Amy Tan / by Susan Muaddi Darraj.
    p. cm.— (Asian Americans of achievement)
  Includes bibliographical references and index.
  ISBN 0-7910-9269-0 (hardcover)
  1. Tan, Amy—Juvenile literature. 2. Authors, American—20th century—Biography—
Juvenile literature. 3. Chinese Americans—California—Biography—Juvenile litera-
ture. 4. Asian American authors—Biography—Juvenile literature. I. Title. II. Series.
  PS3570.A48Z63 2007
  813'.54—dc22   2006026061

Series design by Erika K. Arroyo
Cover design by Ben Peterson

Printed in the United States of America

Bang EJB 10 9 8 7 6 5 4 3 2 1

This book is printed on acid-free paper.

All links and Web addresses were checked and verified to be correct at the time of
publication. Because of the dynamic nature of the Web, some addresses and links
may have changed since publication and may no longer be valid.

CONTENTS

1

The Wake-up Call

During the winter of 1985, Amy Tan was in Hawaii, enjoying a relaxing vacation with her husband, Louis, and her close friend, Gretchen. She especially relished the break from her stressful job—she worked as a freelance writer; her clients were mostly businesses and corporations. She wrote everything from training manuals, business reports, and speeches for company executives for clients that included AT&T and Apple Computer. Though freelance writing was not the employment Tan's mother, Daisy, had hoped for her daughter, it provided a comfortable living and a solid income. The downside of her career was the tremendous number of hours she worked. Sometimes Tan logged as many as 90 hours a week on a project. With all the stress in her life, the vacation in Hawaii was long anticipated and much needed.

Tan was looking forward to the vacation so much that she neglected to leave anyone at home a number where she could be reached while away. One day, while relaxing, Tan received alarming news. Gretchen checked her messages at home and

7

Before Amy Tan began writing fiction, she knew very little about her mother's life.

heard a message that had actually been left for Amy. Her mother, Daisy, had apparently suffered a major heart attack and was in the intensive care unit. The message had been left four days earlier.

Panicked and anxious, Tan rushed to a telephone booth and tried calling the mainland. As she waited to be connected by the operator, she berated herself for being out of touch with her mother and for enjoying the Hawaiian sun while her mother was so ill. As she stood in the telephone booth in the middle of a busy shopping center, still on hold, a terrible memory flooded through her mind.

In her autobiography *The Opposite of Fate*, Tan remembered how years earlier her mother asked her, "If I die, what you remember?" The question was a pointed one: Since Amy Tan was a young girl, she and Daisy had a troubled mother-daughter relationship. Communication was difficult for them, and their few conversations were filled with awkward moments, misunderstandings, and frequent hostility. Tan often reflected that she knew very little about her immigrant mother, a petite woman with a feisty, aggressive attitude toward life.

Daisy's questions also indicated that she realized how little her daughter knew her. Tan reacted to the question with surprise and tried to dismiss it. "Come on, you're not going to die." Her mother continued, asking again, "What you remember?"

At the time, Tan resented the persistence, believing that her mother was trying to make her feel guilty for their disconnected relationship. She failed to answer the question to her mother's satisfaction. At this, Daisy angrily replied, with her heavy accent, "I think you know little percent of me." That conversation now haunted Tan as she waited in the telephone booth for a connection to the hospital. She felt sure that her mother was dead and that she had failed to even try to understand or appreciate Daisy while she was alive.

She offered up a prayer to God and made a vow to spend more time with her mother. "If my mother lives," she recalled saying, "I will get to know her. I will ask her about her past, and this time I'll actually listen to what she has to say. Why, I'll even take her to China, and yes, I'll write stories about her."

Many Chinese Americans are torn between the traditions of their family's birth country and those of their adopted homeland.

Suddenly, the phone connection was made, and someone with a Chinese accent answered at the other end. "Amy-ah?" Relieved at the sound of Daisy's unmistakable voice, Tan began to explain that she thought her mother had had a heart attack. Daisy put her daughter at ease: Apparently, she had argued with the fishmonger at the market. He had tried to cheat her, she believed, and she had become so enraged that she started developing pains in her chest. Self-reliant as always, Daisy drove herself to the hospital. Doctors diagnosed her with angina, a chest pain caused by the heart muscle not getting a sufficient amount of blood; it is usually related to stress. "So you see," Daisy concluded, "That fishmonger, he wrong. Stress me out."

Nonetheless, Daisy was "enormously pleased," as Tan later recalled, that her daughter had been worried about her. "You worry? That's why you call? Yes? Ha, *ha*! You worry for *me*!" she cried gleefully.

As she hung up the phone, reassured that her mother was fine, Tan remembered her vow and decided to live up to it. Later, she described the experience in *Amy Tan: A Literary Companion.* "It was as though somebody had played a cosmic joke on me," she said. She was determined to resolve her long-standing problems with her mother, to know her, so that if she was ever asked again, "If I die, what you remember?" she would have an answer.

Tan wanted to be a good daughter, or at least the kind of daughter her mother expected her to be. She took some of the money she earned from freelancing and bought Daisy a home. She also financed a trip to China for herself and her mother. That trip marked the beginning of a transformation in her life.

As a Chinese American, Tan had always struggled to reconcile the two very different parts of that ethnic identity. Growing up in California, Tan had tried to assimilate into American culture, which meant that she either ignored or neglected her Chinese heritage. She was Chinese at home, where she ate her mother's traditional food, followed the family's cultural practices, and listened to Chinese as spoken by her immigrant parents. Once she left the house, however, she was an American to the rest of the world, and she spoke English fluently, listened to American music, and socialized with her American friends.

Visiting China for the first time with her mother by her side allowed Tan the opportunity to reconnect with her Chinese heritage. It also offered her tremendous insight into her mother's personal life. Finally, it would provide her with the fuel she needed to create a spark in her fiction, which would dramatically impact the American literary scene.

2
Chinese Immigration to America

Most critics agree that the main strength of Tan's writing is the ways she draws on her Chinese heritage and depicts the difficulty of Chinese immigrants adapting to life in America. In fact, much of the material she uses in her novels and short stories comes from the real-life experiences of people in her family or of other people in the Chinese-American community. The history of the Chinese community in the United States is one marked by struggle and difficulty, and that legacy has undoubtedly influenced Tan's work.

Historians divide the immigration of Chinese citizens to the United States into three periods: 1849–1882, 1882–1965, and 1965 to the present. The earliest immigrants arrived after news of the California gold rush had spread to China, and many people flocked to California to seek their fortune. They came with fortune seekers from all over the world, as well as with Americans relocating from other regions of the country. These early Chinese immigrants, who came mostly from the rural Guangdong Province of China, referred to the

Many Chinese immigrants at the turn of the century, like these seen picking cotton in 1907, worked long hours for low wages.

United States as *gum san,* or "the gold mountain." They came to America to make as much money as possible and then return to China. Few returned to their homeland, however.

Most of the immigrants during this period were simple peasants and farmers with a strong work ethic. They worked long hours on the railroads, in mines, on farms, in manufacturing plants, and in lumber camps and slowly built new lives for themselves. These men usually arrived alone, and they sent for wives by ordering "picture brides"—in other words, they agreed to marry based on a young woman's picture; the woman then traveled to the United States to meet her husband and start her new life.

E.D. Huntley, author of *Amy Tan: A Critical Companion*, wrote, "Perhaps because they were the first to arrive, the Chinese formed the largest Asian immigrant group, and they became the first Asians to experience institutionalized discrimination." The Chinese were often denied citizenship and lacked basic civil rights. Many non-Chinese Americans believed that because the Chinese were industrious and willing to work long hours for low wages, they threatened the ability of others to gain employment. In fact, the first wave of Chinese immigration to the United States ended in 1882, when the American Congress passed the Chinese Exclusion Act. This ruling acted on the premise that "in the opinion of the Government of the United States the coming of Chinese laborers to this country endangers the good order of certain localities within the territory thereof."

The effects of the Chinese Exclusion Act marked the second wave of immigration, which lasted in one form or another until 1965. The act banned immigration from China to the United States except in certain, rare situations (some businessmen, teachers, and skilled laborers, for example, were permitted entry).

Most Chinese Americans lived in isolated pockets in American cities; those neighborhoods, largely ghettoes and impoverished areas, became known as Chinatowns. Stereotypes about Chinese people abounded in popular American culture. "[A] number of stereotypical Asian characters became fixtures in certain forms of popular entertainment and literature," wrote Huntley. Two images of Chinese in America dominated: the humble, hard-working immigrant who agrees with everything said to him because he does not speak English and the upper-class Chinese nobleman who possesses great wealth and ancient wisdom. Charlie Chan and Fu Manchu were only some of the stock characters prevalent in American popular culture.

During World War II, the American attitude toward Chinese people changed. It was at that time that Japan, which had also invaded China, became an enemy of the United States. From 1937 to 1945, China and Japan fought what came to be called the Second Sino-Japanese War, in which Japan attempted to acquire Chinese territory. The Japanese military was brutal, as evidenced in November of 1937, when it attacked the Chinese city of Nanking. The civilian inhabitants were tortured and massacred so mercilessly that the event became known as the Rape of Nanking.

The suffering of the Chinese at the hands of the Japanese imperial army won the sympathy of the United States, which also was attacked by the Japanese, during the bombing of Pearl Harbor on December 7, 1941. Suddenly, American attitudes shifted: Japan was the enemy and China was an ally. The Chinese Exclusion Act was lifted in 1943, although limits and restrictions were placed on the number of immigrants allowed to enter the country.

After the war, life for Chinese Americans began to improve. During the 1960s, the civil rights movement in the United States benefited not only African Americans but all Americans who belonged to ethnic and religious minorities that had endured discrimination. Also, in 1965, Congress passed the Immigration and Nationality Act, which abolished the prior system of setting quotas of allowable immigrants from certain countries. Instead, it set a common standard: 20,000 immigrants from all countries in the eastern hemisphere were permitted entry each year, not including special cases, such as children who needed to be reunited with their parents or wives who wanted to join their husbands.

The Immigration and Nationality Act of 1965 sparked the third and current wave of Chinese immigration to the United States. Thousands of people entered the country to be reunited with their families, and many more entered to seek educational and work opportunities. Still others came to the United States to flee persecution or violence. Although in the past, many Chinese had settled in California, immigrants in recent years have established themselves across the United States, mostly in the large cities such as New York, Chicago, and Boston. Immigrants speak Mandarin, Taiwanese, or Cantonese, depending on the region of China from which they hail. As for religion, the vast majority are either Buddhists or Taoists, although some are also Christians.

In her memoir, *The Opposite of Fate*, Tan explained the two major forces that influenced her life: "[I]n my family, there were two pillars of beliefs: Christian faith on my father's side, Chinese fate on my mother's." These two viewpoints of the world were sharply different. "Christian faith," or her father John's perspective, was an orderly vision of the world, whereas her mother, Daisy's, "Chinese fate" led her to believe that life was often chaotic and dramatic, in which nothing was under one's control. Each of her parents' perspectives was the result of life experiences.

John Yuehhan Tan was born in 1913, in Beijing. His father, Hugh Tan, had been Buddhist like most Chinese, but Christian missionaries had converted him at a young age. He embraced his new religion with enthusiasm and zeal. In a sense, Hugh Tan also became converted to the English culture, as well. He attended Western-style schools in China, where he learned to read, speak, and write English flawlessly. In fact, he became literate in English before he could read and write Cantonese, his native dialect of the Chinese language.

Hugh Tan became a minister in the Presbyterian church, and he influenced all 12 of his children to serve the church in some way. As Amy Tan, his granddaughter, later wrote, "The Christian influence ran so deep and strong in the Tan family that all twelve children became evangelists of one sort or another."

This photograph shows the streets in front of Hata-men Gate in Beijing, China, at the time of John Tan's birth in 1913.

John was the eldest of Hugh's children. His mother was a Chinese healer, who believed in traditional Chinese medicines. John resisted the calling to serve the church for many years. His English skills were excellent, though, and during World War II, he worked as a translator for the United States Information Service. In 1941, during the Sino-Japanese War, he was on a boat with his brother, heading down a river in Southwest China, when he met a young woman named Daisy. Although they chatted only briefly, he was attracted to her immediately.

It would be four years before they would meet again. In 1945, John Tan was in Tientsin on assignment when he saw

Chinese schoolchildren learn Christian values at the American Board of Missions in Peking, China, in 1926.

Daisy walking down the street. Though she was married, he picked up where they left off, never anticipating the difficult test their relationship would endure.

Daisy Du Ching was born in 1916. Her mother, Gu Jing-mei, was a beautiful young woman and was happily married to Daisy's father, a scholar. In addition to Daisy, the couple had a son. In 1918, Daisy's father died suddenly from a severe case of influenza; this happened during the worldwide epidemic of the Spanish flu that struck that year, killing 20–40 million people. Gu Jingmei was suddenly widowed at a time when her husband had just started his career. When he died, he had just been appointed vice-magistrate of the county, a promising position filled with potential for success.

One day, in 1924, a rich man with many wives saw the young widow, who was still very lovely. He tricked her into visiting his home, where he attacked her. Shamed by her attack, she felt disgraced and knew that her status in society had been damaged. She saw no choice but to become one of his wives. Her status was not very high within his household, however—she was a "lesser wife," which was even more humiliating. "She was known as the Replacement Wife for Divong, a previous wife whose death Jingmei helped to mourn," explained Mary Ellen Snodgrass, author of *Amy Tan: A Literary Companion*. Gu Jingmei, now a social outcast, left her son behind with her family and took her daughter Daisy with her to live in the rich man's house. His home was located on an island off the coast of Shanghai, where Gu Jingmei and the other wives did not have much contact with the outside world.

A year later, she gave birth to the rich man's son, but one of the other wives, who had a higher status within the household, claimed the child as her own son. Gu Jingmei was devastated. On New Year's Day in 1925, she committed suicide by swallowing raw opium, which she had hidden inside some of the rice cakes for the New Year festivities. She died in front of Daisy, who was only nine years old at the time. Before she died, Gu Jingmei told her frightened daughter, "Don't follow in my footsteps." The young girl became obsessed with death, though, and she spoke often of wanting to kill herself. She missed her mother so badly that, at the funeral, monks tied heavy chains to her ankles "so she would not fly away with her mother's ghost," Tan explained. Daisy never recovered from the loss of her mother.

Story of My Family

DAISY AND JOHN TAN'S LOVE STORY

In her memoir, *The Opposite of Fate*, Amy Tan wrote about the unusual and highly unlikely way in which her parents met and married:

> My father was a latecomer to the ministry, but at the age of thirty-four, he suffered a crisis of morals. A few years earlier, he had fallen in love with a beautiful woman who was unhappily married and had three children. They started an affair, which led to the woman's being thrown in jail for adultery. Shortly afterward, my father left China for the United States, where he had been offered a scholarship to study at MIT.
>
> Upon arriving in San Francisco, he lived at a YMCA and joined the First Chinese Baptist Church on Waverly Street. . . . Through God's prayer he could be granted exactly what he wanted. He prayed that his sweetheart be freed, and sure enough, she was released from prison. Then she cabled my father and asked whether he wanted her to come to America. Shanghai would soon be taken over by the Communists, and his answer had to be now or never. . . .
>
> He may have turned to God also for guidance on how to break the news of his impending marriage to the young women friends he escorted to church picnics and on private outings. . . .
>
> In the summer of 1949, when the minister of his church announced to the congregation that John Tan's bride-to-be was coming from China, several young women gasped and fled the church hall in tears. . . .
>
> My father sent the cable saying, "Yes, come!" to the woman who would be my mother, the Shanghai divorcée who had just been released from prison. And that was how my mother came to the United States and married my father. It was God's will and some other woman's bad luck.

Daisy was returned to her relatives, and she grew up pampered and given everything she needed, but she always felt lonely and disconnected because she had lost her parents. The young Daisy understood that her mother had been in a painful and shameful position when she killed herself, but this knowledge was little comfort. She studied nursing and worked in a hospital in Shanghai. When she was 19 years old, she married Wang Zo, a pilot in the air force. She did not know him very well, as her relatives had arranged the marriage, and Zo turned out to be an abusive husband. He beat Daisy regularly and cheated on her with other women.

Daisy gave birth to a son and four daughters. Unfortunately, her son and one of her daughters died in their infancy, but the other three daughters survived. By 1947, however, Daisy's life was miserable, and she ran away with John Tan, with whom she had fallen in love. In revenge, Wang Zo charged her with adultery and refused to allow her to see her daughters. In China at that time, a woman could be severely punished if she cheated on her husband. Daisy's trial made headlines in Shanghai, and the story of her rocky marriage to Wang Zo became the major topic of gossip in social circles. Daisy was found guilty of adultery and sentenced to a jail term of two years.

John Tan was devastated. As a Christian, he felt guilty that he had entered into a relationship with a married woman, even though she was very unhappy in her marriage to an abusive man. When Daisy was sentenced to jail, he fled China in despair and traveled to the United States, where he had been working as a translator. He was offered a scholarship to the prestigious Massachusetts Institute of Technology (MIT) to study electrical engineering. The calling of the church, which had influenced his entire family and which he had been resisting for years, however, finally persuaded him. He gave up the scholarship to MIT and enrolled at the Berkeley Baptist Divinity School in California, where he studied to be a minister.

A boat on a river in Southwest China in the 1940s, similar to the one on where Tan's parents, Daisy and John, first met.

John mingled with members of the growing Chinese community in California, and many Chinese men thought he would be a suitable husband for their daughters. Like most immigrants, it was important to the early Chinese immigrants in the United States that their children also marry Chinese in order to preserve their language and culture in their new country. Assimilation to the new culture was not as important as remembering their heritage. John was still in love with Daisy, though, and he remained loyal to her while she served her jail sentence in China.

In 1949, Daisy was finally released from prison. China was in a state of civil war, and the Communists were about to seize control of the country. A few days before the borders closed, she fled the country and headed for the United States. The journey to America was a devastating one for her, as she was forced to leave her three daughters behind. Even if she had stayed in China, though, it was unlikely that Wang Zo would have allowed her to see them.

When she arrived in the United States, she met John again and they finally married, eight long years after their first meeting on a boat ride in southwest China. They settled in the area of San Francisco, California, where John continued his ministry with much enthusiasm. He felt that, finally, all the many loose threads of his life had been woven together neatly: He had married the woman he loved, he was working for the church, and they were building a future in a new country. To earn money, he started a business in his home, building small electromagnetic transformers. He also began pursuing his master's degree in engineering.

3

Growing Up Chinese-American

The births of their children fulfilled Daisy and John's ambitions and dreams. In 1950, they had a son, whom they named Peter. In the Bible, Peter was one of the apostles of Jesus Christ, and the one to whom Christ said, "On this rock, I will build my church." No doubt, the Tans had high hopes for their eldest son. On February 19, 1952, the Tans' first and only daughter was born. They named her An-mei Ruth Amy Tan. Her two middle names were given to her in honor of two missionaries whom they knew and respected. Her first name, "An-mei," means "blessings from America," a tribute to their adopted country. Their third child, John, named after his father, was born in 1954.

The Tans expected their children to work hard and excel in school. E.D. Huntley wrote, "The Tans had tremendously high expectations for their children. Amy Tan remembers that from the time she was five or six, her parents articulated clear goals for her: She would become a neurosurgeon because her parents considered the brain to be the most important part of the human body, and during her spare time she would pursue a career as a concert pianist." Early on, it was clear that the Tans wanted their children to have futures that were financially comfortable and culturally expansive.

The children grew up in a solidly Christian home, due more to their father's influence than their mother's. They prayed together at every meal and attended church regularly. John wrote his sermons and read them aloud to his family for their feedback and commentary. Their home was a loving one, although early on, Tan developed a rocky relationship with her mother. Her father was a steady person, who lived each day with enthusiasm and a positive attitude. Part of this was because he had his faith in God to support him. In his diary, he once wrote: "Faith is the confident assurance that something we want is going to happen. It is the certainty that what we hope for is waiting for us even though we still cannot see it ahead of us." He spent as much time as possible with his children, telling them stories and jokes. They rarely went on vacations together, like other families did, because John was always busy working, but the children grew up feeling secure and loved.

Daisy, however, had a very different effect on her children, especially on her only daughter. In many ways, she was the opposite of John, as well as the domineering force in the Tan family. As Tan later wrote about her father, "As smart and strong as he was, he always gave in to my mother's demands." Daisy was an eccentric woman in many ways. Though she was petite and frail looking, her personality was quite powerful and assertive. She was also susceptible to bouts of drama, which made everyone around her tense and hesitant. For example, she believed in ghosts, in the spirits of the dead, and she was certain that they haunted her. The Tan family moved several times when Amy was a child because Daisy would become convinced that ghosts had inhabited their new home. She would become so unhappy and insist on moving that her family, to escape her depressing moods, would acquiesce and find a new home. The family set-tled and resettled in Oakland, Fresno, Santa Rosa, Palo Alto, and other California towns. The near-constant moves resulted in Amy and her brothers resettling at 11 different schools, where they were always the "new kids," who would have to then find a new circle of friends. Tan wrote of that difficult time:

> I had learned to lose friends, to remain the loner until I finally found new ones. Each time I started at a school, I had to sit back quietly for the first month or so and ob-serve who was popular, who was not. . . . I had to show my teachers that I was a good student, that I knew how to draw realistically. But I also knew not to do anything to stand out in any other way, lest I join the ranks of the pariahs. I understood that I had to be a chameleon to survive, that I should fit in quietly, and watch.

Amy became an expert observer of people and their behav-iors, which later contributed to her ability as a novelist to create vibrant, realistic characters.

As a young girl, Amy blamed her mother for these frequent moves and her inability to be allowed to settle comfortably at one school or with one group of friends. As she grew up and became a teenager, her problems with her mother deepened, and their relationship often became hostile. Tan longed for steadiness in her life, but her mother's impulsive and dramatic personality prohibited that. Daisy frequently consulted Ouija boards for advice, and she maintained her belief that ghosts haunted her; she once insisted that Amy herself was the ghost of a dead woman who was angry at Daisy and had come in the form of her daughter to torment her.

As a daughter of immigrants, Tan was trying to assimilate to life in the United States and to American culture. She faced the classic dilemma of children of immigrants: experiencing her parents' culture at home and American culture in the world

Daisy Tan often consulted the spirits through the Ouiji board. Although the board is often laughed off as a game, many people believe spiritual messages can be received through its use.

outside of her home. It was very difficult to grow up with a split culture, and Tan felt that her mother's dramatic personality did not make it any easier.

Growing up Chinese-American was also problematic because of the stereotypes that still abounded about Chinese culture in America during the 1950s and 1960s. Even though America and China had fought as allies during World War II, the Communist takeover of China made the country as hated as the Soviet Union to Americans. The Cold War between America and Communist nations was just beginning, and severe hostility and suspicion existed between them because of their differing economic systems: Communism versus capitalism. In addition to the political problems between China and America, racism existed as well. To the average American in the 1950s, Chinese people "looked different," spoke an exotic language, and ate strange, foreign foods. In American cities, Chinese people tended to cluster together in the same neighborhoods, which became known as Chinatowns, in which street and store signs and other printed materials bore Chinese writing instead of or in addition to English. In American popular culture, Chinese people were rarely featured in movies or on television, except as suspicious, exotic, or silly secondary characters.

Tan grew up feeling torn between being Chinese and desperately wanting to be fully American. She felt embarrassed when friends would come to her home and smell her mother's Chinese cooking. As a young girl, she felt that her features made her stand out from the American girls in her school so she began clamping her nose with a clothespin at night in the hopes of making it smaller. Needless to say, the experiment did not work, but young Amy continued to seek ways to look, act, and feel "American." Often, that meant distancing herself from her Chinese culture as much as possible. This earned her the resentment of her mother.

As a young girl, Amy was deeply unhappy. Her own unhappiness was exacerbated by her mother's violent moods and dramatic depression. At one point, knowing the history of suicide among women in her family, Tan made a half-hearted attempt to kill herself by cutting her wrist with a butter knife. She once told a reporter, "I consider depression my legacy."

To escape her unhappiness, Tan sought the company of books. When she was eight years old, she began accompanying her father once every two weeks to the local library, where she was able to select her own books. She also immersed herself in her schoolwork, and her teachers even recommended that she be allowed to skip a grade (however, she remained with her

Amy Tan developed a love of reading at the Santa Rosa Library. Winning the library's contest made Tan think she could one day write for a living.

class). She read challenging books, beyond the average reading level for her age, and she began forming an opinion about her future: She would like to become a writer when she grew up. She never shared the idea with anyone, because she knew that her parents thought writers did not make much money and would thus disapprove of her choice.

Tan did, however, demonstrate her ability to write well at a young age. In 1960, her third-grade teacher encouraged Amy to express herself through writing. She entered an essay contest sponsored by the Citizens Committee for the Santa Rosa Library. The winning essay, on the subject of "What the Library Means to Me," would be published in the *Santa Rosa Press Democrat*, a local newspaper. Amy won the contest and was awarded with a transistor radio. In her first published work, she wrote:

My name is Amy Tan, 8 years old, a third grader in Matanzas School. It is a brand new school and everything is so nice and pretty. I love school because the many things I learn seem to turn on a light in the little room in my mind. I can see a lot of things I have never seen before. I can read many interesting books by myself now. I love to read. My father takes me to the library every two weeks, and I check five or six books each time. These books seem to open many windows in my little room. I can see many wonderful things outside. I always look forward to go the library.

Once my father did not take me to the library for a whole month. He said the library was closed because the building is too old. I missed it like a good friend. It seems a long long time my father took me to the library again just before Christmas. Now it is on the second floor of some stores. I wish we can have a real nice and pretty library like my school. I put 18 cents in the box and signed my name to join the Citizens of Santa Rosa Library.

Despite her demonstrated ability at a young age to write intelligently and creatively, her parents nevertheless continued to encourage her to think of medicine as a future career. Her brothers, Peter and John, were also encouraged to pursue high-status, high-paying careers.

Her parents' ambitions would be devastated in the spring of 1967. Peter, Tan's older brother, became severely depressed and then suddenly lapsed into a coma. Daisy, ignoring medical advice, insisted that he had become depressed because of trouble he had recently had in school (a schoolmate had copied his report on a novel, causing both students to fail the semester). John, true to his faith, kept praying for a miracle to save his son; he put his trust in God to rescue Peter from the clutches of an

YIN AND YANG

The "yin and yang" is the ancient Chinese theory of opposites, which Amy Tan uses as a structural device in her fiction. In Chinese philosophy, the yin and yang are the two opposing but complementary elements that exist everywhere in the universe, on all levels, such as hot/cold, male/female, fire/water, dark/light, sadness/happiness, love/hate, and other such pairs.

In Tan's *The Joy Luck Club,* the mothers and daughters have a yin/yang relationship: Though they think of one another as opposites, they actually are complementary forces that depend on each other's existence to give meaning to their lives. The daughters, for example, develop their own identities in contrast to those of their mothers. Other dichotomies exist between Asian and American culture, as well as the male and female relationship.

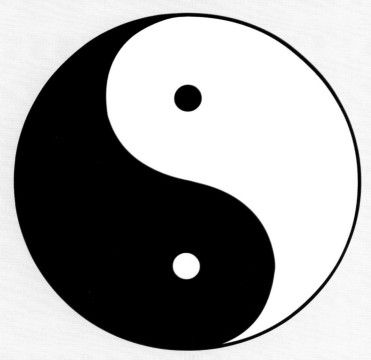

The yin yang symbolizes the ancient Chinese theory of opposites that Tan employs in her fiction.

early death. However, the diagnosis was an advanced brain tumor, which caused Peter's death two months later, at the age of 16. The Tans were stunned by their loss: Daisy felt she was being punished for some past wrong. John could not believe that his faith had not helped his son. Amy, who was in her already difficult teen years, felt more lost than ever.

Soon after the tragedy of Peter's death, his father became ill. John Tan suffered paralysis on one side of his body, which prevented him from writing his sermons. Soon after, the family received the medical diagnosis: Like his son, John also suffered from a large brain tumor. The horrible coincidence threatened to overwhelm the family. Amy watched her father, as she had watched her brother, "waste away" until he resembled a skeleton. In 1968, within a year after his son's death, John was also dead from the same disease. He was only 54 years old.

After the loss of her elder son and her husband, Daisy lost her faith in God. She had been a dutiful minister's wife for years, but now she believed that evil spirits were attacking her family. Relying on her Chinese heritage instead, she consulted mediums and healers. As Snodgrass wrote, "Daisy's explanation of family turmoil was typical of her Chinese upbringing —the Tans and their neighborhood labored under a curse." Determined to save herself, Amy, and her younger son, John, she vowed to find out more about the curse in order to reverse it. Still believing in ghosts, she put the notion in her head that her daughter Amy had the ability to communicate with the dead. She made Amy sit regularly before a Ouija board to try to contact the spirits of Peter and John. The efforts, of course, failed, and Amy was left feeling insecure about her future with a mother who did not seem strong enough to survive the tragedy.

4

The Years in Switzerland

The deaths of her father and brother weighed heavily on Amy's mind. She was still a teenager, suffering from a cultural identity crisis, and she also worried about her own health, her future, and her sanity. Because of the tension that already existed between them, Daisy was unable to comfort her only daughter. The deaths of John and Peter Tan did prompt Daisy to reveal her own tragic past to Amy though. She told Amy about her previous marriage to Wang Zo, about the deaths of her daughter and son, and about how she had abandoned three other daughters in China.

The news that she had three surviving half-sisters in China shocked Amy. The teenager had already suffered so much that she did not react well to this news. She later wrote, "At age fifteen, I was busy finding my own identity. I didn't want to be connected to all this family stuff in China."

Daisy, meanwhile, was convinced that if she remained in California, the bad spirits she could not defeat would claim her other two children. One day, she saw a can of Old Dutch cleanser and interpreted it as a message: she had to take her children to the Netherlands. In August 1968, she, Amy, and John traveled to New York, Washington, and Florida, and then boarded the S.S. *Rotterdam* and sailed to Europe. In Europe, she rented a car and drove her small family to several different countries, waiting for the gods to send her a sign about

Between the Generations

THE IMPORTANCE OF JINGMEI

In *The Joy Luck Club,* Amy Tan recounted the story of a woman who is forced into concubinage, then commits suicide because of the shame her status has brought to her family. The suicide happens in front of her young daughter, who is devastated at the loss of her mother.

In fact, that story is true; the woman was Tan's grandmother, and the young girl was her mother, Daisy Tan. The remarkable change in circumstances from her grandmother's life to her own inspired Amy Tan to reflect on the difference one generation can make in a family's history:

> In my writing room, on my desk, sits an old family photo in a plain black frame, depicting five women and a girl at a temple pavilion by a lake. . . . The solemn little girl is, in fact, my mother. She looks to be around eight. And behind her, leaning against the rock, is my grandmother Jingmei. . . .
>
> I look at that photo [of my grandmother] often, and it's safe to guess that my grandmother never envisioned that she would one day have a granddaughter who lives in a house she co-owns with a husband she loves, and a dog and a cat she spoils (no children by choice, not bad luck), and that this granddaughter would have her own money, be able to shop—fifty percent off, full price, doesn't matter, she never has to ask anyone's permission—because she makes her own living, doing what is important to her, which is to tell

where she should settle down. She finally decided on Switzer-land, where Amy and John could attend a respected, English-speaking school.

The international Institut Monte Rosa, a private boarding school in Montreux, Switzerland, had been founded in 1874. Children from many different countries attended classes there,

stories, many of them about her grandmother, a woman who believed death was the only way to change her life.

A relative once scolded my mother, "Why do you tell your daughter these useless stories? She can't change the past." And my mother replied, "It *can* be changed. I tell her, so she can tell everyone, tell the whole world so they know what my mother suffered. That's how it *can* be changed." . . .

I look at the photograph of my grandmother. Together we write stories of things that were and shouldn't have been, or could have been, or might still be. We know the past can be changed. We can choose what we should believe. We can choose what we should remember. That is what frees us, this choice, frees us to hope that we can redeem these same memories for the little girl who became my mother.

Despite her own troubled relationship with her mother, Amy Tan eventually came to understand that Daisy had served the difficult but crucial role of the transitional generation. She had been the one who immigrated to the United States and raised a daughter in a new environment; she also had the responsibility of infusing her daughter's childhood experiences with as much of the Chinese culture as she could share. Though Amy often thought of herself as caught between two cultures, her mother was in a similar situation: living in a country in which the dominant language and culture were not native to her.

and Amy found herself suddenly in a new, exciting, academic and social environment. Daisy was, by pure luck (although she probably saw it as fate), able to rent a beautiful, furnished chalet overlooking the mountains for only $100 US a month. Amy described it in her memoir: "The largest room served as a living room, dining room, and my brother's bedroom, and its entire length was lined with mullioned windows showcasing a spectacular view of the lake and the Alps. Every day, I would stare at this amazing scenery and wonder how I came to be so lucky. I would then remember that my father and brother were dead, and that was the reason I was here."

Although she had been worried that her Chinese features and culture made her seem odd to classmates in the United States, she realized that her Swiss classmates found her fascinating. "In America," she wrote, "I had been a dateless dork, the sisterly friend to boys I had crushes on. In Switzerland, I was an *exotique*, sought after by the regular customers in the café, the young drifter from Italy, the factory worker from Spain, the radicals from Germany." She began dating a German man named Franz, who enthralled her because he was wild and emotional. Caught up in her own newfound attractiveness and self-esteem, which was based on being considered beautiful and exotic, Amy allowed herself to fall into destructive habits. She began smoking regularly, staying out late at night, and generally rebelling against her mother in every way possible.

Though the family was in Switzerland at her own insistence, Daisy began thinking that it had been a terrible mistake. She was isolated in Switzerland more than she had even been in the United States, and to make things even worse, Daisy felt that she was losing control over her children. She was especially convinced that Franz, who did not have a job and hung out in cafés all day playing table soccer, would destroy Amy's life.

Despite her rebellious nature, Amy continued working hard in school and was a straight-A student. She had also begun applying to colleges and thinking about future careers. Even without her mother's constant warnings and complaints about Franz, Amy sensed that she needed to end the relationship. Shortly before her final examinations, she tried to break up with him. Franz dramatically threw himself on the nearby train tracks and threatened to let the next train slice him in two unless Amy agreed to elope with him at that moment. Terrified, Amy agreed, calling her mother from the train station to inform her that she was running away to marry Franz.

Daisy was more resourceful than her teenage daughter realized. Not too long after, she showed up at the train station, accompanied by the Swiss police, who stopped the two lovebirds. Although the episode caused her to fail her final exams, Amy clung to Franz more than ever, not because she really loved him, but because she was furious at her mother's interference. Daisy, realizing that she had to save her daughter from the destructive relationship, hired a private detective to investigate Amy's German boyfriend.

The detective discovered many secrets about Franz. While he had told Amy that he had deserted the German army, it turned out that he had actually escaped from a mental institution in Germany. Furthermore, he was a small-time drug dealer. The detective reported to the authorities that Franz and his friends were dealing drugs, and so they were arrested and deported. Amy herself was dragged before a judge and made to swear that she would not befriend drug users again. She also vowed to stop behaving badly: "I had to . . . promise I would not do anything bad ever again in my entire life. I would not smoke, not even one cigarette. I would always obey my mother, give her not even one word of defiance." (It appears Daisy may have had a conversation with the judge before the court date.)

Despite her ability to rescue her daughter in difficult situations, Daisy herself still exhibited destructive behavior. At one point, overwhelmed with the task of raising two teenagers by herself in a foreign country, she threatened to kill herself and her children and end it all. She and Amy had been fighting about Amy's rebellion, and Daisy wanted her to understand that she was ruining her life. She told her daughter during the fight, "I rather kill you! I rather see you die!"

During this terrifying incident, she held a meat cleaver to Amy's neck for 20 minutes, and Amy truly thought her mother would kill her:

> She slammed the door shut, latched it, then locked it with a key. I saw the flash of a meat cleaver just before she pushed me to the wall and brought the blade's edge to within an inch of my throat. Her eyes were like a wild animal's, shiny, fixated on the kill. . . . For ten minutes, fifteen, longer, I straddled these two thoughts—that it didn't matter if I died, that it would be eternally sad if I did—until all at once I felt a snap, then a rush of hope into a vacuum, and I was crying, I was babbling my confession: "I want to live. I want to live."

Though she discovered a sense of her own beauty there, the years in Switzerland had been traumatic and filled with emotional upheaval. When Amy graduated from high school, Daisy moved the family back to California, where at least she had friends, a support system, and could speak the language to some extent.

Once back in California, Tan enrolled in Linfield College, in Oregon. She had received an American Baptist Scholarship, and Linfield was a Baptist institution with a conservative reputation, which her mother liked. Daisy expected her daughter to become a doctor. Such high expectations were daunting to Amy, who did not feel that she wanted a career in the medical field. More specifically, Tan's mother wanted her to specialize in neurosurgery, or brain surgery. It had been a brain

Amy Tan attended Linfield College, a Baptist institution in Oregon.

tumor that had killed her father and brother, a coincidence not lost on Amy. She had always nurtured the dream of becoming a writer, but she knew that such a career choice would be frowned upon because it did not garner a high income. According to her mother's wishes, she enrolled in premed courses at the college.

To earn extra money, she worked part-time at a pizzeria. She tried to go out and have fun with her friends, but her studies were demanding and exhausting. One evening, her friends set her up on a blind date with Louis DeMattei, an Italian-American student who was pursuing a degree in law. They fell deeply and quickly in love. One afternoon, shortly after they met, they drove to San Juan Bautista, a deserted town with a lot of history. There, they happened upon a wedding taking place, and the bride and groom insisted they join in the festivities. After the celebration, the two lay down on the grass and stared up at the sky, and Tan wrote that, at that moment, she felt she had found her true love.

They started dating exclusively, although DeMattei's parents were alarmed by their son's choice of a girlfriend. According to Snodgrass, "Daisy, an impressive combatant at four-feet-nine and eighty pounds, came to her daughter's defense by confronting the DeMatteis." Tan was surprised that her rescuer was the one person with whom she constantly fought, but the experience also proved to her that her mother did, indeed, love her.

More battles with Daisy awaited her, however, despite this show of confidence. In 1970, Tan decided to leave Linfield College and enroll at San Jose City College to be closer to Louis. Though she and her mother had been mending their relationship (Amy had even begun to study Mandarin Chinese, which pleased Daisy enormously), this move caused a major rift between them. In addition, Tan decided that she would no longer pursue a medical career; instead, she decided to major in English and linguistics. Daisy, disappointed and upset, refused to speak to her daughter for a long time.

In 1972, Tan, who transferred again to San Jose State University, graduated with a double degree in English and linguistics. She enrolled at the University of California in Santa Cruz to pursue a master's degree in linguistics. After finishing her master's degree in 1973, she enrolled at the University of California, Berkeley campus, and began her studies at the doctorate level. This placated Daisy, who thought that, if her child would not be a medical doctor, she would at least have a doctorate degree in an academic field.

Amy Tan met her future husband Louis DeMattei (pictured at a Rock Bottom Remainders Show in 2006) through friends she worked with at a local pizza parlor.

That year, she also married Louis, who had graduated recently himself and was working as a tax lawyer. The young couple struggled financially, but they were happy. They both worked hard at their careers, taking odd jobs to add to their incomes. At one point, they both worked at a pizza parlor part-time, where they met Pete, a young student at the university who was also employed there. Pete was a bioengineering student whose wife had died in a car accident years earlier; he spoke about her lovingly to Amy and Louis. Before long, Pete began renting a room in their apartment. This was an ideal way for Amy and Louis to decrease their expenses and to spend time with a good friend.

They enjoyed their time with Pete. The three young people often worked late shifts together and spent many hours talking and getting to know one another. They also had many adventures: At one point, a gang had started trouble in the pizza parlor, and the three had thrown them out. The gang had vowed revenge against them and attacked them twice.

Despite the fact that her pursuit of a Ph.D. pleased her mother, Tan had begun to have doubts about her academic choices. She realized that she had only enrolled in the Ph.D. program after graduation because she had had no other ideas at the time. She had no clear direction in her life and no sense of ambition. Feeling lost, she signed up for the program and pursued her studies half-heartedly. That feeling changed dramatically in February of 1976.

A New Career

The gang of thugs that had attacked Amy, Louis, and Pete was still causing trouble. They contacted the police, but they were told that, although members of this gang were known to be troublemakers, they could not be arrested. The three friends decided to move to another town, to escape the death threats they were receiving. Pete moved to Oakland, and Louis and Amy waited to get an apartment in the same building as their friend.

On her twenty-fourth birthday, Tan spent the entire day out with Louis, and they did not return to their apartment that night. The day after, Tan received a phone call from another friend who lived in Oakland, in the same building as Pete. The friend delivered devastating news. "Pete's dead. Two guys broke into his place last night and killed him," he said.

Tan's initial response was denial. "That is the worst joke I've ever heard," she replied. Unfortunately, it turned out to be the terrible truth. Two men—apparently not the gang members who had been threatening them for so long—had broken into Pete's apartment at night. They had knocked him over the head with his own gun (which he had purchased to protect himself) and tied him up so that the same length of rope connected his neck and ankles. The result was that he strangled to death.

The killers then used Pete's gun to shoot at the door of the apartment manager. They also shot and killed a young college student who happened to be standing outside as they made their getaway by car.

Because Pete's family lived in Wisconsin and could not arrive quickly, Amy and Louis had to go to the Oakland Police Department headquarters to identify their friend's body. The experience was shocking to both of them. They could not believe that their young friend, so hopeful about the future despite the loss of his wife, had been murdered in such a cruel, barbaric manner.

Tan's mother had always believed in ghosts and in the power of dreams, but Tan herself had never put much faith in these things. The night after Pete's death, though, she sat in her apartment with her husband and a group of their friends, talking about their friend and grieving together. Tan, who had drunk a lot of alcohol to drown out her sorrow, suddenly felt Pete's presence in the room. "I heard Pete's voice," she later wrote. "By that I mean that it sounded as if he were speaking out loud. It was no doubt grief preying upon my imagination, drunken thinking taking voice. Yet I could not help relaying aloud what I had just heard: 'The names of the guys who killed him are Ronald and John.'" Tan's husband and friends felt sorry for her, believing that her misery had finally affected her deeply enough so as to cause hallucinations. She insisted, however, that she heard Pete's voice clearly telling her the names of his murderers.

A few days later, two men were arrested as they tried to rob a store in Oakland. In the back seat of their car, police found several items that they had stolen in previous robberies, including an expensive calculator they had taken from the apartment of a bioengineering student named Pete a week earlier. The names of the two men were Ronald and John.

Shortly after the incident of Pete's death, Tan began suffering from what Snodgrass explained is psychosomatic laryngitis, "a self-silencing at the thought of an unspeakable crime." In fact, every year on the anniversary of his death, she found herself unable to speak, to even utter a single word. This continued for seven years.

Tan also began seeing him in her dreams. Although she had always dreamed in vivid detail since she was a young child, she had never placed much importance on the meaning of those imaginings. In her dreams of Pete, however, her murdered friend gave Tan advice about her life and her future; he told her

SAN FRANCISCO BAY AREA

The San Francisco Bay Area, comprising the cities of San Francisco, Oakland, San Jose, and other, smaller cities, is home to 8 million Californians, making it one of the largest metropolitan areas in the United States. Surrounded by water on three sides, the region is known for its cool and foggy, but generally pleasant, weather. What most distinguishes the San Francisco region from other urban centers, however, are its unique ethnic characteristics.

The city has one of the nation's oldest Chinatown neighborhoods, which forms a backdrop for much of Tan's fiction, as well as a Japantown and other concentrations of Filipinos, Vietnamese, and other Asians. An Italian community in North Beach, a French Quarter, and Irish and Russian communities in the Richmond District further enhance the city's rich ethnic landscape.

Amy Tan and husband Louis DeMattei live in the famous historic neighborhood known as The Presidio, which overlooks the San Francisco Bay.

to believe in herself, in her abilities and talents, and to directly confront any fears that she held. "The dreams may have been delusional," she later reflected, "the result of emotional trauma at having seen the gruesome evidence of a friend's death. Yet even if that is the case, it does not diminish the importance of those dreams to me or what I learned and did as a consequence."

Pete's messages to her, transmitted through the medium of her dreams, encouraged Tan to drop out of the doctoral program at the University of California, Berkeley. She justified her decision by insisting that not many jobs were available for people with a Ph.D. in linguistics; plus, her energy and enthusiasm had never been invested fully in the idea of earning a doctorate. Instead, she applied for and got a job at the Alameda County Association for Retarded Citizens, working with children who had severe disorders and learning disabilities.

She helped children and their parents develop their language skills. The job proved to be a real learning experience for her. Many of the parents with whom she consulted believed their children had the ability to learn and grow, even when the disability was something as severe as Down syndrome or another disorder. "Over the next five years," Tan writes, "I had opportunities to work with more than a thousand families, and from them I sensed the limitlessness of hope within the limits of human beings. I learned to have compassion. It was the best training I could have had for becoming a writer."

In 1980, after a move with Louis to San Francisco, she began directing a project for children with developmental disabilities. She thrived on having a positive impact on the lives of challenged children. Despite the fact that her career as a language development specialist was vastly fulfilling and satisfying, Tan became disturbed by a trend that she noticed in her workplace. She would often be tapped to serve on a committee, council, or task force because, as a member of an ethnic minority, she was told, her perspective would be valuable. She felt, however, that she was becoming a token minority representative. "What bothered me was . . . that they would think that one Chinese American could represent American Indians, and blacks, and [Hispanics]. Chinese Americans are very different from immigrants . . . from Thailand and Cambodia and Vietnam," she later said. For that and other reasons, she quit the job and decided that she would finally do what she had wanted to do all along: write.

Writing creatively full time was out of the question, because it would not pay the bills. Further, as a novice writer, she had no guarantee that magazines and journals would even accept her stories for publication. Instead, she focused on technical and business writing, which paid quite lucratively.

Tan started out with a few small clients, but eventually she included major corporations such as AT&T, Bank of America, and IBM among her contracts. For these companies and others, she produced a wide range of documents and reports, including training manuals, speeches for the CEOs and directors, memorandums, brochures, and other materials. Her work consumed her, demanding long hours, although the flexibility was a definite benefit. As a freelancer, Tan could set her own hours and work out of her home a vast majority of the time.

Ethnic stereotyping continued to hound her even in her new career, however. When she wanted to disguise the fact that she was Chinese American, she even changed her name on her documents, writing under the pseudonym May Brown.

The money she was earning was more than she had ever hoped, and she and Louis were able to live a very comfortable life. Daisy was also pleased that her daughter was doing so well financially. The level of stress in Tan's life increased, however. Her hours became longer and longer as she took on more projects, working, at times, almost 100 hours a week. She began to suffer from depression and to see a psychiatrist. Her sessions were not very successful, and she realized, at one point, that

Amy Tan began a successful freelance career writing business and technical speeches, manuals, and presentations.

they were even detrimental because the therapist was not show-ing much interest in or sympathy for her problems: "I would talk about feeling good, and he'd fall asleep. But if I recalled something from my childhood that was traumatic, and I was crying, he was very attentive. And I thought, he's reinforcing me to be unhappy."

This destructive trend of working long hours and seeking unhelpful therapy continued until the day in Hawaii when Tan thought her mother had suffered a heart attack. When she heard that her mother was all right, she decided that something in her life had to change—and it had to change dramatically.

She stopped attending therapy sessions and forged her own form of therapy: She sought relaxation in more creative and productive ways. With her husband and friends, she began playing music. She had been trained to play the piano as a child and had enjoyed her lessons. Now she found an outlet for her stress in playing with an amateur jazz band. She also did something that would later influence her ultimate career choice: She began reading contemporary literature, especially by women writers.

Some of her favorite and most influential writers included Eudora Welty, Alice Munro, and Flannery O'Connor. Many ethnic women writers also influenced Tan, who was just beginning to write creatively. She learned that she could write about culture and ethnicity in a way that was illuminating and insightful.

For example, Tan was intrigued by the novels of Isabel Allende, who wrote *The Stories of Eva Luna*, *The House of the Spirits*, and *Daughter of Fortune*, all of which are novels. She also wrote memoirs, including *Paula*, which is about her relationship with her ill daughter. Allende's novels feature the Latin-American style of magical realism, which is a way of writing in which fantastical events are related in a straightforward, direct manner. Tan was no doubt reminded of the way her mother related amazing stories of her own life and childhood in a similarly straightforward manner.

Tan also became a fan of Louise Erdrich, a Native American writer who authored such works as *The Game of Silence*,

Chilean author Isabel Allende's work, specifically her use of magic realism, served as an inspiration to Tan.

The Last Report on the Miracles at Little No Horse and *The Painted Drum*. Tan was most interested in *Love Medicine*, a collection of stories about Native American characters in which the plot lines are linked and the characters of one story appear in another. The stories revolve around several generations of two large families who live on a Chippewa reservation in North Dakota.

In an interview, Tan once credited *Love Medicine* as being the book that sparked her idea for a similar book based on Chinese American characters. "I just loved that book," she said, "and thought, 'Hmm, maybe I can write a number of stories linked by community.'" In her memoir, *The Opposite of Fate*, she also said, "*Love Medicine* is the book that made me want to find my own voice. It influenced my early attempts to write fiction." So, Amy Tan began to write.

6

Honing Her Craft

Tan's first short story was entitled "Endgame." The subject matter was one that she knew quite well: a young Chinese girl who is a chess wizard, but who has trouble dealing with her mother. Through the process of writing the story, Tan tried to find her own voice, inspired by the strong and poignant voices of her favorite fiction writers.

Though the story was not perfect and would be reworked, it did achieve the voice that Tan was struggling to craft. She submitted it as part of an application to the Squaw Valley Community of Writers, a workshop taught by Oakley Hall, the author of historical novels such as *Warlock* and *The Coming of the Kid*. Hall, who also taught at the University of California at Irvine, wrote several books on the craft of writing, especially fiction writing and crafting the novel. He was a superb first writing teacher for Tan, and, when she enrolled in his workshop, he recognized her talent right away.

During that workshop, Tan met other writers, including Molly Giles, who later went on to publish such fictional works as *Iron Shoes, Creek Walk and Other Stories,* and *Rough Translations.* She also met Amy Hempel, who went on to write *Reasons to Live, The Dog of the Marriage,* and *At the Gates of the Animal Kingdom.* They encouraged Tan to continue writing fiction and offered her solid advice on how to improve her work. Hempel told her, she recalled, to "look for the news in my story, and to go for the things that are the most uncomfortable."

During the course of the workshop, Tan revised "Endgame" and, when she felt that it could not be improved upon any further, she sent it out for publication. Most writers receive a stream of rejections from publications for years before they are accepted and break into print, but *FM Five* accepted her story, and *Seventeen* magazine reprinted it.

Tan began working on a second story, entitled "Waiting Between the Trees," also about Chinese American themes. When it was finished and had been reviewed by the members of the workshop, she mailed it to the *New Yorker* magazine, one of the most prestigious cultural magazines in the country. The magazine rejected Tan's story.

When the workshop ended, the experience had been so inspiring and exhilarating that several members wanted to continue to meet and learn from one another. Molly Giles, who had already won prizes for her writing, including the Flannery O'Connor Award for Short Fiction, agreed to lead the writer's group. She became Tan's friend and mentor in the journey to develop as a writer.

Tan's stories were rich in detail, because they were often based on true events in her own life. However, one of the biggest influences—and sources of material for her fiction—was Daisy. After Daisy's hospitalization, Tan resolved to spend more time with her mother and to learn about her. That is when Daisy began to tell her daughter stories about her own childhood in China, her first marriage to Wang Zo, and about the five other children she had, including the three daughters who were still alive. Tan was stunned by the amazing life her mother had lived, and perhaps even more stunned that she had never known about it. Mistakenly, she had assumed that her mother

CULTURAL REVOLUTION

After World War II, China was devastated by the Japanese assault and tried desperately to recover both culturally and economically. The Communist Party, led by the visionary Mao Zedong, was swept into power in 1949. Mao later became a power-hungry dictator. Amy Tan's half sisters grew up during this time.

In 1966, Mao launched a movement known as the Cultural Revolution, intended to help China reemerge as a powerful nation. The program trained the country's youth to follow a uniform way of thinking and behaving—based on Mao Zedong's teachings—and to make the glory of the greater nation their main priority. It was a radical social experiment that would affect China's future.

During the Cultural Revolution, schools were shut down and urban youth were mobilized into small army-like units called the Red Guards. The Red Guards were encouraged to revolt against anyone who was not loyal to Mao's way of thinking; they were also taught lessons from "philosophy" texts written by Mao himself.

Many people who were considered disloyal were attacked and sometimes killed by these youth. Millions were forced into camps, where they were doomed to years of manual labor, although others were executed by a government that was, by this point, a mere puppet of Mao Zedong.

Before long, China was drowning in a sea of political instability and social chaos. The Cultural Revolution ended with Mao's death in 1976, but it left major problems in its wake. The biggest problem was that an entire generation of young people were without an education and without means to function in a new China, in which education and political process were emphasized.

Daisy Tan lived through the military buildup in China. Shown here are provincial troops marching along a city street in China in 1946.

had always been the person Tan had known her to be. Now, she was learning all about the person her mother had once been.

As Tan listened to her mother share stories from her life, she understood for the first time that she had neglected her relationship with Daisy. As Huntley wrote, "Amy began to realize that she did remember fragments of stories from her childhood, bits and pieces of her mother's reminiscences, images and episodes from tales about life in China. As a matter of fact, she was

surprised to discover that she did have a considerable—if imag-
istic and impressionistic—knowledge about Chinese culture."

Tan started to understand how her mother was shaped by
the tragedies she endured. While researching one of her stories, Tan needed more information about what life was like in
China during the Second Sino-Japanese War and World War II.
She asked her mother if she had been affected by the wars; her
mother replied, "War? Oh, I was not affected." Tan asked her to
remember what had been happening around her at the time.
Daisy began to recount what she remembered: "[S]he began to
tell me details of their life in China—of bombs falling, of running to escape, of pilot friends who showed up for dinner one
week and were dead the next."

Confused, Tan asked her mother why she'd said earlier that
she had not been affected by the war. "I wasn't," said Daisy. Then
she clarified: "I wasn't killed." For her, being "affected" meant
being killed; such a view of life and death could only be shaped
by someone who had seen much tragedy and destruction and
considered herself lucky to have lived through it.

The more she talked to her mother, the more Tan realized
how little she knew about her. She decided to live up to the
promise she made in Hawaii: to take Daisy to China. It would
be an opportunity for Daisy to see her family and friends, and
especially her other three daughters, and for Tan to see and
experience the country of her ethnic origin.

Tan made plans to fly to China with her mother in 1987.
Before she left, however, her friend and mentor Molly Giles put
her in touch with Sandy Dijkstra, Giles's own literary agent.
Dijkstra read one of Tan's stories and asked to see more; Tan
did and was pleased with the agent's suggestion that she as-
semble them into a book. Tan had wanted to write a collection
of linked short stories ever since she had read Louise Erdrich's
Love Medicine.

Communist Party leader Mao Zedong's portrait hangs above Tiananmen Square.

The trip to China, she thought, would be an excellent way to collect more material to fill out the collection. In October, she and Daisy flew to Shanghai. Tan was hesitant about the journey because she wasn't sure what to expect on her first visit to China. She was also secretly worried that perhaps her mother, upon reuniting with her other "Chinese" daughters, would suddenly find Amy inadequate.

Tan was stunned, however, to find that she felt comfortable and at home in China almost immediately. Her family members in China, whom she had never met, were hospitable, open, and loving toward her. She was surprised at how much Chinese she was able to speak and how much she also understood. Her three half sisters, Daisy's surviving children from her first marriage, also welcomed Tan warmly, and the reunion was a wonderful experience for all of them.

Tan also learned about how difficult life in China could be. At this time, China was just emerging from the Cultural Revolution. In 1976, Chairman of the Communist Party Mao Zedong died, thus ending the 10-year social experiment he had started. The Cultural Revolution mobilized Chinese urban youth to organize themselves into small armies dedicated to the vision of a unified, antielitist nation, following the vision set forth by Mao. It quickly lapsed into a violent, corrupt movement that did not advance China, but rather set it back by decades.

When she returned to the United States, Tan was exhausted—emotionally, physically, and mentally—from all that she had experienced during the trip. She was a new person, much changed, and she needed time to absorb and contemplate all that had happened. She was not to have that time, however. Shortly after her return, Sandy Dijkstra contacted her with exciting news. A publisher wanted to buy Tan's book of short stories.

Writing
The Joy Luck Club

Sandy Dijkstra gave Tan the details: Six different publishers had made offers on the idea of a book of Tan's stories, all featuring Chinese and Chinese-American characters. The tentative book title was *Wind and Water*. The winning publisher, GP Putnam and Sons, paid an advance of $50,000 against the royalties she would make on the book's sales. There was only one problem: Tan had not yet finished writing the book. As she later said, "It was like winning the lottery when I hadn't really bought a ticket!"

The news was exhilarating and exciting, but after Tan's initial happiness subsided, her suspicions arose. What if the publisher only wanted a book about Chinese and Chinese-American characters as a way to put a novel about ethnic or racial minorities on its booklists? She decided not to worry about those fears and to focus instead on writing the book for which she had already been paid.

Amy Tan finished her remaining business writing by the beginning of 1988 and focused full-time on writing the rest of the stories that would go into the book *Wind and Water*. She employed much of the material learned from conversations with her mother, as well as details of her recent visit to China. She wrote every day from a desk in her basement, while listening to the music of Kitaro, a Japanese musician, and burning aromatic incense sticks. By doing so, she created an atmosphere that spurred her imagination and helped her to focus her mind on the task at hand.

Tan created four main characters, all young Chinese-American women growing up in the same neighborhood. June "Jing-mei" Woo is a struggling freelance writer who fears that her mother is disappointed in her lack of achievements; Waverly Jong is a former child chess prodigy who marries a non-Chinese man; Rose Hsu Jordan is still emotionally insecure after a childhood incident in which she failed to rescue her brother from drowning; and Lena St. Clair Livotny suffers from a crippling lack of self-esteem inherited from her own mother's wild sense of fear and despair. Each young woman is plagued by a difficult relationship with her immigrant Chinese mother; the cultural and generational gaps conspire to prevent the mothers and daughters from forming a strong, close friendship with one another. Tan decided to tell some stories from the points of view of the daughters and some stories from the points of view of the mothers. In this way, she sought to explain how each side viewed the other and to explore the experiences that shaped both generations of women.

As Mary Ellen Snodgrass wrote in *Amy Tan: A Literary Companion*, "Tan completed the text by pretending that characters were visitors telling their stories." She also relied on the Chinese tradition of *talk story*. Critic Linda Ching Sledge defined this technique in the following way:

[A] conservative, communal folk art by and for the common people, performed in the various dialects of diverse ethnic enclaves and never intended for the ears of non-Chinese. Because it served to redefine an embattled immigrant culture by providing its members immediate, ceremonial access to ancient lore, talk story retained the structures of Chinese oral wisdom (parables, proverbs, formulaic description, heroic biography, casuistical dialogue) long after other old-country traditions had died.

In Tan's work, talk story is evident in the way in which the Chinese immigrant mothers of Rose, June, Waverly, and Lena

TALK STORY

The Chinese talk story is a long-established form, but one that—like most forms of oral storytelling—was only recognized recently in the United States as a type of art. Talk story is the way in which one generation passes down its wisdom, experiences, and history to the next. The term can be used as a noun, as in "Talk story is a significant art form," or as a verb, as in "Children grow up listening to their parents and relatives talk story."

In Chinese culture, a talk story, which is similar to a folktale or a fable, was generally shared between mothers and their daughters. Therefore, it was an art form in which women, rather than men, participated. For example, in *The Woman Warrior*, the influential memoir by Chinese-American writer Maxine Hong Kingston, the author refers to her mother's talk stories often. These talk stories were the bits of wisdom, wrapped in the package of an interesting story, that held a lesson her mother wanted to make sure her daughter learned.

The lessons of the talk stories could be moral, social, or cultural in context. Often, the talk stories taught the women of the younger generation how to survive and maintain their identity as Chinese women in a challenging society.

try to communicate with their Americanized, English-speaking daughters. They desperately want to pass on to their daughters elements of the Chinese culture and tradition that they themselves have a difficult time maintaining because they are now living in a different country. The daughters, on the other hand, know little about Chinese tradition except for a few stories and some old, wise sayings. Talk story is the mothers' means of sharing their own experiences with their daughters.

Tan finished the book four months later in the spring of 1988 and she gave the completed manuscript to Sandy Dijkstra. When she read it, Dijkstra felt that the title should be changed from *Wind and Water* to *The Joy Luck Club*. In the short story collection, the four mothers gather periodically to play a popular Chinese game called mah-jongg. The idea of a "Joy Luck Club" was formed by Suyuan Woo, the mother of June Woo, who had originally started a mah-jongg club in wartime China with friends to pass the time during air bombing raids. The purpose of the club back then was to preserve the participants' hope for some joy and luck in their seemingly doomed futures. Suyuan recreated the club in California with her other Chinese immigrant friends to form a community of friends in a new country where everyone felt alien and alone. In Tan's work, Suyuan Woo is recently deceased, and so her daughter June Woo is asked to take her mother's place in the Joy Luck Club—this serves as a symbol of all that June has inherited from her mother, as well as a link between the two generations of women.

The book went into production in early 1989, and Tan was thrilled to know that Louise Erdrich, among other writers, had endorsed it. When the book appeared on bookshelves in 1989, Erdrich's words on the back cover read: "Amy effortlessly mixes tenderness and bitter irony, sorrow and slicing wit. *The Joy Luck Club* is a fabulous concoction."

The Joy Luck Club rapidly climbed the charts and by April 1989 was officially a best seller. It remained on the best seller list

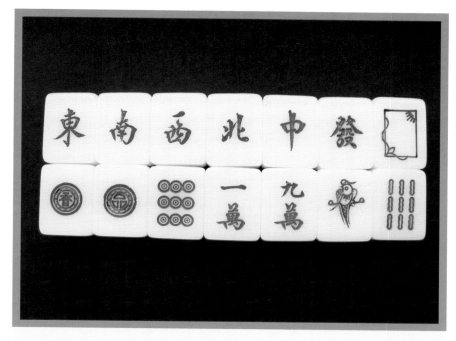

The characters in *The Joy Luck Club* use their time playing mah-jongg to bond and talk about their dreams.

for 34 weeks, until another publisher paid more than $1 million for the rights to issue it in paperback form. It was published in 25 languages and sold in other countries very well.

The short story collection won several awards, including an American Library Association Best Book for Young Adults award, and was nominated for the *Los Angeles Times* Best Book of the Year prize and the National Book Critics Circle's Best Novel of the year awards. The book was also a finalist for the National Book Award that year.

The outpouring of admiration from Tan's new fans flooded in. Many people, especially Chinese Americans, felt that the book spoke personally to them. Many mothers believed that it helped them better understand their daughters, and daughters felt that the book gave them insight into their mothers' lives and experiences. Others were amazed by the skillful way in which Tan created a distinct voice and circumstance for each of the characters and related new insights about life in the United States for Chinese immigrants and their families.

Although *The Joy Luck Club* earned Tan much praise, it also garnered some criticism, mostly from Chinese-American writers and critics. According to Snodgrass, "A handful of exacting Asian-American critics dismissed the work as dumbed-down Orientalism suited to Caucasian readers." Snodgrass cites such criticisms: *The Joy Luck Club* is "comforting [to whites] in its reproduction of stereotypical images and . . . Orientalist fantasies of Old China." Snodgrass also mentions writer Frank Chin, who charged Tan with falling into the trap of depicting Chinese culture as patriarchal and oppressive to women.

Other ethnic writers have faced similar charges from members of their own communities. Decades ago, when Asian culture was not well understood by Caucasian Americans, stereotypes abounded about these countries and their people. A popular myth was that China still lived in a medieval era, when emperors ruled, people lived luxuriously in grand palaces, servants were treated harshly, and men married more than one woman. Indeed, most movies made in the United States and Western countries about Asia featured these hallmarks, which were outdated and generally false notions of what life was like in modern China. This is an example of Orientalism, the label used to describe this stereotypical view of Asian countries. Orientalism paints Asian cultures as universally oppressive of women, or misogynistic.

Three of the mothers featured in *The Joy Luck Club* grew up in China during the war and often relate stories of their own childhood. Lindo Jong, who is clever and assertive, tells of how she was forced into an arranged marriage and lived in the house of her husband's family. Oppressed and subjugated, especially by an overbearing and demanding mother-in-law, she outwitted her in-laws to escape from the marriage. An-mei Hsu recounts how

The actresses who portrayed the mothers and daughters in the movie adaptation of Amy Tan's book *The Joy Luck Club*, formerly known as *Wind and Water*, pose on the set of the popular movie.

her mother was forced to marry a rich man who had attacked her and compromised her reputation. To escape from this marriage, her mother ate raw opium, which she had concealed inside some food. (This story is, of course, based on the real story of Tan's grandmother, Gu Jingmei.)

Critics of Tan felt that these stories seemed to substantiate an Orientalist view of Chinese culture. Tan had no intention of depicting Chinese culture in an Orientalist manner—she was only telling stories that she had heard growing up. When Maxine Hong Kingston published her best-selling memoir, *The Woman Warrior*, she was also charged with painting an Orientalist picture of Chinese culture.

The truth is that all cultures have dark periods in their history, but to write about those times does not mean that a writer hates or is trying to falsely depict that culture. At the same time, other writers have portrayed the culture wrongly in the past, which makes some people, like Amy Tan's critics, more sensitive to these depictions.

Another criticism of *The Joy Luck Club* was the way in which Tan made the mothers in the stories speak English with an accent. Some felt that she was allowing the reader to poke fun at Asian immigrants and their inability to speak fluent English. "Using the mother to tell of her life in China," wrote one critic, "has deprived Tan of the full resources and muscularity of the native English-language speaker."

Tan was surprised by the criticism of her work from people in the Asian-American community, and it made her think about what type of a writer she was and wanted to be. In an essay entitled, "Required Reading and Other Dangerous Subjects," she addressed this issue. She wrote:

> If I had to give myself any sort of label, I would have to say I am an American writer. I am Chinese by racial heritage. I am Chinese-American by family and social upbringing. But I believe that what I write is American fiction by virtue of the fact that I live in this country and my emotional sensibilities, assumptions, and obsessions are largely American.

In other words, Tan does not want to be labeled as any type of ethnic writer. Instead, she feels that she represents what the United States itself represents: the idea that a country can embrace people of all nationalities, religions, and backgrounds under one flag. Likewise, her writing is informed and inspired by her racial background and upbringing, but it is a uniquely American blend.

Tan went on to say in her essay that she does not believe that critics should tell Asian American writers what to say and *how* to portray Asian culture. Although some Chinese American women, for example, may have never experienced oppression, some have, and both stories are legitimate. There is no one single way to portray any culture, and to insist that there is means that one is suddenly not able to write freely.

Furthermore Tan added that she does not believe in the notion that Asian-American writers should be responsible for portraying Asian culture in a positive manner. "I can only suppose that if writers were responsible for people's thoughts and for creating positive role models, we would then be in the business of writing propaganda, not art as fiction. Fiction makes you think; propaganda tells you how to think."

In response to the charge that having the mothers in *The Joy Luck Club* speak in accented English made them look silly, she insisted that she allowed the mothers in the stories to speak because they are so often silenced by virtue of the fact that they are immigrants in a new land. "My own mother has long been deprived of telling her story," she wrote, "this story, because she lacked those native English-language skills."

One thing she realized quickly, after the success of *The Joy Luck Club*, as she went on an exhaustive book tour, was that she was being asked by interviewers and readers about issues not related to fiction. Suddenly, people wanted her to talk about political and social issues related to China and to the Chinese community in the United States. These questions reminded her of how she had been used as a representative, a token minority, in the past when she worked with children with learning impediments—and she did not want to experience that again. Thus, she refrained from replying to these questions and limited her answers to queries about writing, fiction, and her characters. Then, Amy Tan focused on her next book.

8

The Sophomore Effort

Writing her second book—which was her first novel, because *The Joy Luck Club* was actually a short story collection—proved to be a daunting task. *The Joy Luck Club*'s success was the stuff writers dream about: an immediate best seller that makes literary ripples around the world. Tan could not hope to match that success—she only wanted to prove that she was capable of maintaining her writing style through a second, sophomore effort.

The success of *The Joy Luck Club* was so vast that it intimidated and threatened to overwhelm her. How could she duplicate such an achievement? In an essay entitled, "Angst and the Second Book," she began by writing, "I am glad that I shall never again have to write a Second Book." She described how she fretted over what people, especially other writers told her, such as "The Second Book's doomed no matter what you do," and "How does it feel to have written your best book first?"

She began to suffer from depression and a psychosomatic condition that caused her to break out in hives; she also developed neck pain and a severe case of jaw pain, which caused her to grind her teeth while she slept and crack two of her teeth. Back pains, which forced her to put hot packs around her waist whenever she sat down to write. She also developed writer's block, which she overcame by working on speeches and other assignments instead of actually tackling the Second Book.

Tan had to shut out all interruptions in order to write the book. Discipline had never been a problem for her, and so she isolated herself for a time and focused on the work at hand. She had several false starts, which she described in her essay:

> In between my bouts of back pain, jet lag, and guilt, I did start writing my Second Book, or rather, my second *books*. For example, I wrote eighty-eight pages of a book about the daughter of a scholar in China who accidentally kills a magistrate with a potion touted to be the elixir of immortality. I wrote fifty-six pages of a book about a Chinese girl orphaned during the San Francisco earthquake of 1906. I wrote ninety-five pages about a girl who lives in northeast China during the 1930s with her missionary parents. I wrote forty-five pages about using English to revive the dead Manchu language and the world it described on the plains of Mongolia. I wrote thirty pages about a woman disguised as a man who becomes a sidewalk scribe to the illiterate workers of San Francisco's Chinatown at the turn of the twentieth-century.

By her own estimation, Tan wrote almost one thousand pages in false starts on the second book. The process was grueling and disappointing, but she needed it to find her way to what she really wanted to write about.

TWO DISTINCT CULTURES

Amy Tan views herself as a Chinese American. In other words, she is an American woman with Chinese racial heritage. The two halves of her ethnic identity are both central; one cannot wholly represent her. Instead, she sees herself, as the children of many immigrants do, as the product of the merging of two very distinct and different cultures. She speaks Chinese to her family in China and enjoys home-cooked Chinese food, for example, but she also sings American rock music in a band called the Rock Bottom Remainders.

There is no doubt, however, that her Chinese heritage informs and influences her writing career. Most of her fiction has featured Chinese and Chinese-American characters. Even her nonfiction often focuses on what it is like to grow up as the daughter of Chinese immigrants in America.

In her heritage, she has tapped into a rich source of material, which shapes her stories and infuses them with vivid and illuminating detail. She has often directly used the experiences of her mother, Daisy, to create her plots and characters. The story of Winnie, in *The Kitchen God's Wife*, for example is exclusively the story of her mother's torturous and abusive first marriage. Her frequent visits to China to visit relatives, to conduct speaking engagements, or to promote her writing are considered "research trips" by Tan, who often uses details and experiences gleaned from these travels in her writings.

Although she feels comfortable being identified as a Chinese-American or an Asian-American writer, Amy Tan rejects being made a token of that culture. From her work experience in San Francisco, she has become sensitive to the ways in which Americans of minority cultures (Asian Americans, African Americans, and others) are often used to represent entire communities. She does not ever pretend to know what the Asian-American community as a whole thinks, because, as she would say, there is not one uniform opinion that the community holds. To ask one person to represent that community is to fail to understand that multiple opinions and perspectives exist within it.

Therefore, as a Chinese-American or Asian-American writer, she follows the age-old wisdom offered to writers: "Write what you know." She creates characters and stories that are usually based on real-life experiences of her own family, and she writes about feelings she felt growing up in the United States as a Chinese American. Her novels have been noted for their specificity of details, which she mines from the lives of her own relatives or the stories that have been passed on to her. In this way, she recovers and explores stories—usually those of the women in the family—that have never before been considered, because their subjects were often dismissed as unimportant or frivolous. *The Kitchen God's Wife* is one example.

In another example, she remembered a story her mother had once told her about a woman who escaped the Japanese invasion, and during her flight and long walk to safety had to shed her belongings one by one because they became too heavy to carry. Tan revamped this story in *The Joy Luck Club* as the tale of Suyuan Woo, who had to leave her belongings by the side of the road during her escape, until she was forced to abandon her twin daughters, as well.

Tan does not assume that all Asian Americans will be able to relate to her work, because they may not have shared her experiences. She writes what is true not for the Asian-American community, but what is true for Amy Tan.

The character Suyuan Woo in *The Joy Luck Club* is based on the real-life experiences of Tan's mother, Daisy, who left her children behind in China.

Once again, Tan turned to her mother for inspiration. She had always been intrigued by her mother's first marriage, which Tan found out about when she was an adolescent. Her mother had been abused both physically and emotionally by Wang Zo, her first husband. She had only escaped the situation when she left China for America, where she married John Tan. She had paid a steep price for her escape, however, in that she had to leave behind her three daughters. Tan used this story as her starting point. She allowed herself to imagine what life had been like for her mother in that disastrous marriage. She explored the feelings and experiences of her mother and other characters in the situation.

Once she found her voice, she worked diligently on the Second Book, spending hours at her desk working and drafting the novel. She took no phone calls and refused all requests to speak at conferences, give interviews, and other distractions from the actual work of writing.

The result was *The Kitchen God's Wife*, which was published in 1991. Critics had been suspicious of Tan's second effort, as most writers do struggle with their sophomore attempts after a successful first book, but Tan showed them that her initial success was no fluke.

Many consider *The Kitchen God's Wife* her finest writing. Snodgrass referred to it as a "Chinese *Gone With the Wind*" because of its scope and range. In the novel, a Chinese-American woman, Pearl Louie Brandt, learns of the first marriage of her mother, Winnie Louie. The relationship between mother and daughter is filled with tension, especially after the death of Pearl's father, Winnie's second husband. Winnie, however, reveals to Pearl the story of her past, her childhood, young adulthood, and unhappy first marriage to Wen Fu, an air force pilot who treated her brutally. By writing the story of Winnie, Tan tells the true story of her mother Daisy, and finally allows her own mother to share her tragedy with others. As she told an interviewer, "[My mother] wanted someone to go back and relive her life with her. It was a way for her to exorcise her demons, and for me to finally listen and empathize and learn what memory means, and what you can change about the past."

The Kitchen God's Wife climbed to the top of the best seller list within one month after its release, and it remained there for several more weeks. It won the *Booklist* Editor's Choice Award, and it was translated into several languages. Some critics insisted that Tan had once again portrayed Chinese culture as misogynistic and in line with the Orientalist stereotype that Chinese men are abusive and Chinese women are oppressed.

Most readers, however, praised the book's emotional impact and carefully crafted prose style. Indeed, the style itself is a tribute to Daisy, as Tan wrote it in a very simple way so that her mother would be able to read the book easily, without stumbling over complicated language.

Readers also praised the way in which Tan offered insight into the lives of Chinese Americans, as well as of Chinese living in mainland China:

> Amy Tan re-creates the intricately textured world of the Chinese American community, a world that encompasses San Francisco's alive and bustling Chinatown neighborhoods as well as the China of over half a century earlier, a homeland that that exists only in the memories and stories of the older generation.

With the success of *The Kitchen God's Wife* behind her, Tan embarked on a new and different type of adventure: She wrote a children's book. Her friend Gretchen Schields joined her in the effort. Schields was an illustrator who had spent many years growing up in Asia, specifically in China, and she agreed to illustrate Tan's text. For the story line, Tan returned to the story of Ying-ying St. Clair, the mother of Lena St. Clair, in *The Joy Luck Club*. In one episode of that first book, Ying-ying relates how, as a child in China, she once fell off her parents' boat and into the lake during the celebration of the Moon Festival; later, she encountered a woman known as the Moon Lady. In the children's adaptation of this story, a little girl, also named Ying-ying, disobeys her parents and her nanny, but she is taught a lesson by the Moon Lady. She learns not to be selfish and to respect her family and others. The book, entitled *The Moon Lady*, garnered praise for its story and Tan's ability to flex her writing talents and adapt her style for younger readers.

Tan found the popularity of her books enormously gratifying. After the publication of *The Joy Luck Club*, she and Louis moved into a condominium in San Francisco's elite Presidio

Scott Turow and Amy Tan performing in costume with Rock Bottom Remainders, a group of high-profile authors who play concerts to benefit writing programs.

Heights, where the windows offered a view of the Golden Gate Bridge and the San Francisco Bay. More important for Tan, though, it offered a comfortable place for her to relax and write. Success also came with a price, however: The demands on her time put a strain on her energy and stress level.

To relax and to unwind, she joined fellow writers in a makeshift band that called itself the Rock Bottom Remainders. Formed by Kathi Kamen Goldmark in 1991, it featured writers Stephen King, Barbara Kingsolver, Dave Barry, Louise Erdrich, and others. The group performed only once or twice a year, but for Tan, the experience of singing onstage, often in costume, provided not only comic relief but also another means of creative expression.

She was soon to have yet another medium in which to express herself. In 1991, she found out that *The Joy Luck Club* was to be made into a feature film. June Woo, Waverly Jong, Lena St. Clair, and Rose Hsu Jordan, as well as their mothers, were about to hit the big screen.

9

The
Silver Screen

"I was an unlikely person to get involved with filmmaking," wrote Tan in her memoir, *The Opposite of Fate*. In 1991, however, a proposal was made that *The Joy Luck Club* be made into a feature film.

At first, Tan was hesitant to allow the book to be made into a movie. After all, the characters were mostly incarnations of herself. In creating them, she had given them her own fears, dreams, idiosyncrasies, and personalities. How would this translate to the big screen?

At a screenwriting workshop in 1988, before her first book was published, Tan had heard horror stories from writers whose books had been made into films: "One novelist-turned-screenwriter was still gnashing his teeth in regret. They had taken his literary novel, trampled it with pat formulas. . . . Later, he had to endure watching the movie with an audience that included his squirming literary friends, all of whom developed simultaneous coughing fits."

IMPORTANT ASIAN AMERICAN WRITERS

Although Amy Tan is not the first Asian-American writer to become a household name, she is certainly one of the more famous. Other writers, however, have also contributed to the growing genre of Asian American creative writing.

Maxine Hong Kingston, the author of *The Woman Warrior: Memoirs of a Girlhood Among Ghosts,* has been a tremendous influence on Amy Tan and other writers. Born in 1940 to Chinese immigrant parents, Kingston was awarded a scholarship to the University of California, Berkeley campus, where she excelled in her studies. She spent years teaching English in private schools, both in Hawaii and in the United States. Her memoir was published in 1976, to great critical acclaim. The sequel, *China Men*, appeared in 1980 and won the National Book Critics Circle Award. In 1989, Kingston published her first novel, *Tripmaster Monkey: His Fake Book.*

Shirley Geok-lin Lim is an award-winning poet and fiction writer as well as a critic. Born in 1944 in Malaysia, she was abandoned by her mother and grew up as the only girl in a family of five boys. Her childhood was marked by poverty and hardship, and she was struck by the fact that she was unable to find an adequate outlet to express herself. She persevered in her studies, where she found comfort and solace in studying literature, and her efforts were rewarded by a scholarship to the University of Malaya. Later, fellowships enabled her to complete her Ph.D. in English in the United States. Her poetry collection, *Crossing the Peninsula and Other Poems*, won the Commonwealth Poetry Prize in 1980. In 1990, she (along with coeditors Mayumi Tsutakawa and Margarita Donnelly) won the American Book Award for *The Forbidden Stitch: An Asian American Women's Anthology.* She published a highly acclaimed memoir, *Among the White Moon Faces: An Asian-American Memoir of Homelands*, in 1996. She has published

Author Maxine Hong Kingston reading from her book *The Fifth Book of Peace* in 2005.

collections of her short stories, and, most recently, a novel entitled *Joss and Gold*, which appeared in 2001.

Jessica Tarahata Hagedorn was born in 1949 in Manila, in the Philippines. Her childhood was filled with difficulty because she grew up during the era when Ferdinand Marcos ruled the Philippines. Her family escaped and emigrated to the United States in 1960, where Hagedorn spent her formative years, studying music and acting at the American Conservatory Theatre. Hagedorn writes in many different genres, including poetry, novels, plays, and other forms; she has also experimented as a performance artist and as a musician. She has published several collections of poetry and short fiction, and her novel

(continues)

(continued)

Dogeaters was nominated for the 1990 National Book Award. She also founded the West Coast Gangster Choir, a rock band. Her novel *The Gangster of Love* appeared in 1996. Hagedorn most frequently writes about the difficulties people trapped between cultures experience. She discusses anti-Asian racism in the United States but also critiques the Filipino-American community for its own problems with class inequity and other issues.

Marilyn Chin, a poet, was born in Hong Kong in 1955 but emigrated to the United States as a child with her family. She spent her formative years in Portland, Oregon. Upon arrival in the United States, her father changed her name from Mei Ling to Marilyn (after Marilyn Monroe), so that she would have less difficulty assimilating to American culture. Her sister was renamed May Jayne, for the actress Jayne Mansfield. Chin's poetry collection, *The Phoenix Gone, the Terrace Empty* appeared in 1994. *Dwarf Bamboo* appeared in 1987, and *Rhapsody in Plain Yellow* was published in 2002. She often writes about the difficulty of adjusting to a new culture, as well as growing up between two very different cultures.

Shortly after *The Joy Luck Club* was published, Tan's agent, Sandy Dijkstra, began receiving inquiries from movie producers about the possibility of making the best seller into a film. Dijkstra signed on a film agent to help negotiate with the producers. Over the next few months, they received several offers, but Tan turned them down. She still was not willing to allow her characters to be turned into two-dimensional figures on a movie screen.

In August of 1989, a few months after the novel's initial release, Tan met director Wayne Wang, who spoke with her at length about being Asian American. He helped put Tan's worst fear—that a movie would portray Asian Americans in a stereotypical, negative way—to rest. Feeling comfortable with Wang, Tan agreed to join forces with him and allow him to direct a movie based on her book and her characters.

About that time, Tan also met screenwriter Ron Bass. He presented her with several intriguing ideas for how to translate a book, which was essentially composed of several short stories and many lead characters, into a coherent film. "The book could succeed as a movie, he said, only if we broke all the rules," Tan recalled. He wanted to keep all the characters, as well as to use voiceover to help smooth the transitions between time and generations.

With Wayne Wang and Ron Bass, Tan agreed to be a co-writer as well as a coproducer of the film. Being part of the team made her feel more invested in the film's success and gave her a way to protect and watch over the transformation of her book's characters into movie figures. In this manner, she could make sure that, from start to finish, the movie version of *The Joy Luck Club* remained true to the original idea and meaning of her book.

The idea for the screenplay was soon sold to Hollywood Pictures, part of the Disney company, which gave them a $10.6 million budget. The trio jumped into their project with enthusiasm. Filming began in the fall of 1992 and would last more than a year. During that time, Tan felt that she was enrolled in a hands-on crash course about moviemaking.

The process of writing a screenplay was grueling, but Tan had excellent teachers in Ron Bass and Wayne Wang. She described the work sessions the trio held:

> The process of collaboration turned out to be, much to my relief, more like a relay race than a three-legged one. It fit my work style perfectly—to be engaged in intense creative discussions first, then allowed to go off and write by myself. Between drafts, Ron and I would meet

with Wayne to get his take on how the script was going. It was important that the three of us be in alignment at every step. We were on the phone with one another almost daily. Our collaboration was so thorough that by the time we saw screenings of the movie, we often could not remember who had written what.

When filming began, there were more lessons to be learned. Tan even received two small acting parts in the film: in one, she is dressed in a 1940s outfit, and in the second, she and Ron play a husband and wife arriving late to a dinner party. As the filming went on, many small changes had to be made to the script, so Tan was on call for these last-minute edits. She learned how a script evolves and develops along with the film itself.

In 1993 Tan flew to China with the cast and crew to film the scenes set in China. The experience of filming scenes in Chinese villages, using local people as extras in some cases, was fascinating to Tan. In one anecdote, which she recounted in her memoir, Tan recalled how the crew had to use a little resourcefulness to keep the filming on schedule:

On the day we were to film refugees fleeing an invading Japanese army, the people living in our location were holding a funeral for a woman who reportedly lived to be a hundred before she died. It was either bad luck or bad manners—probably both—for them to allow a film crew into their village that day. The procession was long; obviously, this ceremony was going to take hours. A casket was being carried, and dancing on top was a live rooster, supposedly to chase off evil spirits like movie directors, cast, and crew. But to delay shooting

Amy Tan with actress Annette Bening and director Wayne Wang after a screening of the motion picture *The Joy Luck Club* in 1993.

even one day would cost us $70,000, money we could ill afford on our budget. Discussions were held with the family, a generous "donation" was made in honor of the dead woman, and suddenly, the gods smiled upon us. The film crew was welcomed and the villagers rejoiced at the infusion of cash. The old woman, we overheard, had brought her comrades good luck.

The reactions to *The Joy Luck Club* were positive. Audiences of all ethnic and racial backgrounds felt the impact of the powerful, interwoven stories of the Chinese and Chinese-American women. Tan was especially nervous about how Daisy would react to the film. After viewing it, Daisy calmly told her daughter,

"Pretty good. In real life, everything so much sadder. So this, already much better."

In 1994, Tan began working on a new project, a second children's book, with Gretchen Schields again as illustrator. She also was busy writing her third novel, *The Hundred Secret Senses*. For this book, she once again turned to her family history. Rather than write about mother-daughter relationships, as she had in *The Joy Luck Club* and *The Kitchen God's Wife*, Tan focused on the relationship between sisters in her new book. The sisters in the novel are Olivia Bishop, the daughter of a Chinese father and an American mother, and her half sister Kwan, who was born in China and immigrates to the United States as a young woman.

Literary critic E.D. Huntley wrote, "Readers familiar with Tan's work will immediately recognize in *The Hundred Secret Senses* a number of distinctive Tan trademarks: a strong sense of place, a many-layered narrative, family secrets, generational conflict, Chinese lore and history, and an engrossing story."

What is different in *The Hundred Secret Senses* from past novels, however, is that Tan also experimented with supernatural elements; the Chinese sister, Kwan, believes that she is gifted with the ability to communicate with the dead, which upsets and concerns her American half sister. The novel was published in 1995, and it received generally positive reviews, although some critics felt that the ending was weak and some felt that Tan's focus on the supernatural was stilted and not believable.

The publication of her book also brought up the issue of how she was classified as a writer. For years, Stephen King, Tan's friend and partner in the Rock Bottom Remainders music group, had been complaining that writers like him were being unfairly categorized as genre writers. The controversy had been brewing for a long time as to whether writers are "literary writers" or writers of popular fiction—the

Best selling horror writer Stephen King appears with Amy Tan at the 2002 New Yorker Festival in New York City.

demarcation between the two categories was never made clear. King believed that just because a writer's works sold millions of copies and had a large fan base did not lessen the integrity or the quality of the work. In other words, he and others, like Tan, were not "dumbing down" their fiction to appeal to a larger readership.

In 1996, Tan had an experience that made her understand that reading and writing are forms of freedom. In March of that year, she traveled to China to participate in an event that would raise funds for Chinese orphaned and disabled children. She was to speak to a group of more than 450 guests, including ambassadors and international businesspeople. The speech was canceled by the Chinese government's Public Security Bureau an hour before it was scheduled to take place. The reason given was that the group did not have the required permit to hold a fundraising event, but the real reason, as most suspected, was that Tan had planned to talk about censorship by the Chinese government.

Amy Tan had always been aware of censorship and the lack of freedoms in China, but the problem became of special concern during the Tiananmen Square massacre, which took place in September of 1989. In that incident, the Chinese government ordered its troops to fire on Chinese students who were demonstrating peacefully for greater freedoms and rights. The event shocked the world and caused people around the globe to scrutinize more closely than ever the ways in which China's citizens were being silenced and suppressed.

Tan continued to work hard and write, while also finding time to relax with her husband, Louis. The two had agreed that they would not have children. Because her own childhood had been so erratic and her relationship with her mother so troubled, Amy felt she would have a difficult time being a mother. The couple's relationship was very fulfilling: They were best friends, and they supported one another's endeavors.

They also took many adventures together. In the winter of 1997, they spent some time vacationing with their friend Jan in their cabin near Lake Tahoe, in Nevada. A fierce rainstorm kept them inside most of the time, but they became worried when the rain did not subside after five days. On New Year's Day, they realized that the Truckee River was swelling. Soon afterward, they knew they were in danger: The rain had melted a heavy snow, causing flooding and mudslides. They called for help, and the local sheriff's office dispatched rescuers in three separate trips to save them. Wearing lifejackets and helmets, Louis, Amy, and Jan, as well as friends from a neighboring cabin, were floated in a raft across the flooded area to the safety of the riverbank. The rescuers also saved Amy and Louis's pets and Amy's backpack. In the backpack was her laptop, which contained part of her latest novel.

During this time, Daisy's health had been steadily declining. She had been having hallucinations in which she saw the dead and predicted the future. At one point, she insisted that she had seen O.J. Simpson kill his wife, Nicole Brown, during the height of the infamous murder case and ensuing trial. In 1995, doctors officially diagnosed her as having Alzheimer's disease, which causes a rapid deterioration of one's memory. Tan had already noticed that her mother had grown more and more forgetful over the years, and that she had gone through bouts of angry and violent mood swings, so the diagnosis was not much of a surprise, but it was still a shock.

Tan felt that it was her duty to take care of her mother in her last days, although it was hard to watch her mother decline because, as she said, "My mother had always bragged about her memory. She never forgot anything." Now, however, she was forgetting people's names and suffering from many delusions. At one point, she called Amy several times a day, insisting she could prove that Louis DeMattei was having an affair and that Amy had to leave him.

Author Amy Tan speaks all over the country, including this 2002 engagement at the civic center in Syracuse, New York, as part of the Rosamond Gifford Lecture Series.

Though her mental health had been deteriorating for years, in 1999, Daisy's physical health became dramatically worse. In her last conversation with Amy, Daisy apologized for all the hurt she had caused in Amy's life and asked her to try to forget the difficult times. Tan felt that this reconciliation was important, and she was grateful for her mother's candor and honesty.

Tan's three half sisters flew in from China to be present, along with Amy and John Tan, Jr., at Daisy's death, which occurred on November 22, 1999. Toward the end, Tan felt relieved, because even though her mother's forgetfulness had been painful to watch, she realized her mother had also forgotten many painful experiences, such as the deaths of her brother Peter and her father in the late 1960s. She was also happy that after 47 turbulent years, she and her mother had finally made peace with one another.

10

Living
With Loss

Nevertheless, Tan was not to realize how deeply the loss of her mother affected her until she lost someone else who was close to her. As with the deaths of Peter and her father, Tan was once again fated to lose two people within a short period of time. Her editor, Faith Sale, died on December 7, 1999, of cancer. Like Sandy Dijkstra, Sale had helped usher Tan into the world of literary publishing and had been a great friend and mentor.

At Faith's memorial service, Tan delivered a short speech, recounting how much their friendship had meant to her. "I remember the proudest moment I had as her friend," Tan said. "We were at a medical clinic, and Faith was having her blood drawn. The nurse looked at Faith, then scrutinized me and said without any hint of the absurd, 'You two are sisters, aren't you?' And Faith looked at me without any hint of the absurd and said: 'Yes. Yes we are.'"

Tan began writing her next novel, *The Bonesetter's Daughter*, but she could not focus on the writing process. She

Actors Dennis Yen and Tina Huang perform in a production of Tan's short story "Immortal Heart," presented on stage by San Francisco's Word for Word Performing Arts Company in 2004.

suffered from fatigue and memory loss. She consulted several doctors, who could find nothing wrong with her, so she continued working on her novel, secretly worried about her health. *The Bonesetter's Daughter*, as she later told the press, was her most personal publication because it traces the lives of two narrators, a mother and daughter, and their struggle to resolve their relationship. The mother suffers from dementia, and Tan even recounted in the novel's last chapter the last conversation she had with her mother, in which Daisy asked her forgiveness. The novel was published in 2001 and once again, the critics praised it for its raw emotion and moving storyline.

After a four-month tour to promote the book, which sold very well, Tan's physical health was in jeopardy. She felt completely exhausted and fragile. Even more frightening was her lack of motivation to do anything.

Anyone who had a schedule like Tan's in 2001 would have complained of exhaustion. She had recently completed a book tour that lasted four months and took her to 40 cities in the United States, as well as to Europe and Australia. In addition, she was still emotionally recovering from the deaths of her mother, Daisy, and good friend and editor, Faith Sale. In between, she was working on several new projects, including a children's television show she was writing for PBS. For Amy Tan, who had always been a hard worker accustomed to long hours and packed schedules, though, the level of fatigue she felt was not normal.

She complained to her husband that her body felt broken. She slept poorly, waking often throughout the night because of a strange vibration throughout her body that seemed to emanate from her bones. In addition, she could not concentrate on her writing long enough to finish anything substantial, and reading proved a taxing chore. She also suffered from memory loss. A blood test showed that she had dangerously low blood-sugar levels, but doctors were puzzled as to what could be causing it. A brain scan even showed that she had several lesions on her brain, but thankfully, she did not have a tumor (a secret fear she had harbored, given the fact that her father and brother had both died of brain tumors). The mystery continued, though, and "I found myself wishing for a diagnosis," she wrote, "which in essence meant I was wishing for a disease."

New symptoms appeared every day. Her hair began falling out in clumps, her speech sometimes became incomprehensible, and she could not drive easily because of the decline of her reflexes. She also began suffering from hallucinations. Once she imagined that her husband Louis was dead and his ghost had visited her in the middle of the night; another time that two girls played next to her bedside, skipping rope; and even that a corpse was lying next to her on the floor. The hallucinations terrified her, because she felt that she was losing control, and she began acting irrationally and erratically as well. In the absence of a real diagnosis, she feared that medical experts would begin to think that she was simply going insane.

Then, a doctor prescribed more testing for her to rule out more unusual diseases, such as Lyme disease. Upon seeing the word "Lyme" scribbled on a medical form, Tan remembered that years earlier, she had found ticks on her dogs and had had them tested for Lyme disease. She had never thought to have herself tested, though, because she had never seen a tick on her own body. She researched the symptoms of Lyme disease on the Internet, and sure enough, found that the range of symptoms included fatigue, low blood sugar, insomnia, disorientation, inability to concentrate, and even thinning hair!

Tan began a grueling round of antibiotics, which worsened her symptoms over the next two weeks. As the medication took effect, though, she gradually began to feel better. Two months later, her energy level returned to normal, she was able to resume her usual activities. Her motivation and her spirits were greatly improved.

Tan wrote about her experience with the disease in the final essay of her memoir, "The Opposite of Fate," which bore the same title. *The Opposite of Fate*, a collection of several of her personal essays, was published in 2003 to great critical acclaim. Once again, she proved that she could write across genres, whether it was fiction, children's fiction, or nonfiction. The essays depicted many of her personal struggles, with her mother, with her writing, and with life's challenges, to her wide readership and fan base.

She continued to work on developing a children's television series for PBS, and with friend Gretchen Schields, who illustrated her previous children's books, she created *Sagwa: The*

In 2005, the Lyme Disease Association hosted Literati with Lyme, a fundraising event entitled "Writer's Block of the Worst Kind," featuring writers who have had Lyme disease. Amy Tan; Meg Cabot (*The Princess Diaries*); E. Jean Carroll (advice columnist for *Elle* Magazine); Jordan Fisher Smith (*Nature Noir: A Park Ranger's Patrol in the Sierra*); and Jennifer Weis (executive editor St. Martin's Press) all participated in the event.

Chinese Siamese Cat. The half-hour animated show, set in ancient China, features the adventures of Sagwa, a winsome cat who is eager to explore and learn new things. Music and fairy tales complement the show's storyline. Tan wanted the show to be a positive way to educate young American children about the rich and varied culture of China.

Although in the past she shunned becoming a spokesperson for any political agendas, in recent years, Tan has become more politically vocal. In 2003, the United States declared war on the government of Iraq. Along with several other writers, Tan protested the war, insisting that there was not enough justification for the United States to go to war. On March 20, 2003, she and 144 other people signed their names to a full-page advertisement in *The New York Times*, declaring their opposition to the invasion of Iraq. It was already a tense time in the United States and in the rest of the world, where antiwar marches and demonstrations were held regularly to protest the action. In the United States, however, those who opposed the war were often viewed as "anti-American." Tan did what she had always done, though: She followed the path that seemed right to her.

Her protest of the Iraq War parallels her involvement in protesting the censorship and strict authoritarian regime of the Chinese government. One of her half sisters moved to the United States with her husband and family, and from that sister, Tan learned about how difficult life really was in her parents' native country. Since then, she has given her time and energy to help alleviate the hardships of people living in China and to help resolve their problems, whether from poverty or lack of freedom. In *The Opposite of Fate*, she wrote about this issue:

> As Americans, we have an inordinate fondness for rights. Our country was founded on them; we enjoy the right to bear arms, to bear children, to bare our thoughts as we see fit. The right to life, the right to choose, the right to die, the right to speak out or remain silent. We argue ferociously for our rights in whatever way each of us interprets them. When we do it on out own soil, we are on solid ground. We have lawyers who can back us up. But when we argue for rights on behalf of people in another country, things get a bit tricky. They don't always go the way we intend.

Later in the essay, Tan asked, "So what should we do about human rights in China?" The answer, she beliveed, is not to try to "teach" Chinese people about their rights or to fight on their behalf against their oppressors. Instead, she asked that we attempt

MAH-JONGG

An ancient game, mah-jongg is played with tiles, which are arranged competitively by the players. The game requires four players; an appropriate symbol for the characters in *The Joy Luck Club,* in which June Woo must take the place of her deceased mother, Suyuan Woo, in order for the game to continue.

Mah-jongg requires a symmetrical arrangement of the tiles, similar to the author's arrangement of the various stories in *The Joy Luck Club.* The game is a casual one, but the women play competitively, which often reveals how, despite their friendship and companionship, they do compete in other ways. (Lindo Jong, for example, consistently holds her daughter Waverly above her friends' daughters, lauding Waverly's many achievements. The women also compete with one another regarding their cooking skills, each believing her food to be the best.)

The older generation in *The Joy Luck Club* plays mah-jongg as a way to pass the time but also as a vehicle to converse and share their stories with one another. Suyuan Woo forms the original Joy Luck Club during the war. She gathers other refugees to play the game as a way to talk about their hopes and wishes for security and to bring some joy in their seemingly bleak lives. In America, Suyuan again organizes a Joy Luck Club among her fellow female Chinese immigrant friends who have daughters whom they are trying to raise in this new and alien culture.

Snodgrass wrote, "There is more to games of mah jong than passing the time with friends. Before the women's emigration, conversation provides an outlet to Chinese females whom rigid patriarchy, polygymy, and male-centered feudal marriage stifled."

to open the lines of communication between ourselves and these people. Although she hopes the politicians have broader and more effective ideas, she wrote, "What I can do is give money for cleft-palate surgeries. I can fund fellowships so that foreign journalists can study in the United States and take fundamental ideas back to their own countries. I can provide assistance to Tibetan groups developing self-sustaining industries." In these small ways, she believes greater change can take effect.

In 2006, Tan published a new novel, her fifth. *Saving Fish from Drowning* explores new territory in Tan's development as a writer. Rather than write about generational conflicts in the Asian-American community, as she did in past books, her new novel follows the adventures of a group of American tourists lost in the Burmese mountains. The force behind the narrative, however, is the dead Bibi Chen, who was one of the original travelers.

In the prologue to the book, Tan informs the reader that the story she created is actually based on something that may have been true. During an unintended visit to the American Society for Psychical Research, Tan stumbled upon the writings of Bibi Chen, a San Francisco socialite, as transcribed by a psychic medium named Karen Lundegaard, who had been "visited" in various sessions by the spirit of the dead Chen. Intrigued, Tan met with Karen and interviewed her about the experience.

"Karen had transcribed Bibi's voice in pencil on yellow legal pads. This began as spastic marks and jerky false starts, then gave way to pages of frantic squiggles and drunken scrawls, and gradually loped into the smooth shape of handwriting," said Tan. In these transcribed writings, Chen explains how she traveled with some spoiled American friends through Burma, where their journey encountered several dangers and challenges.

"However these writings came to be, I decided the material was irresistible," added Tan. She used it as a starting point for her novel, which is unlike anything she had ever written before.

Amy Tan participates in the 2002 New Yorker Festival on September 28, 2002. The festival brings together writers, artists, critics, and speakers to celebrate excellence in the arts.

For one thing, it required a lot of research, especially about the country of Burma, known also as Myanmar, which borders India to the southeast. Furthermore, the adventures are narrated by the deceased Bibi Chen, whose ghost follows her friends.

Reviews of *Saving Fish from Drowning* were mixed. Some critics praised the novel for its detail and experimental format, whereas others bemoaned Tan's decision to move beyond her usual subject matter.

Tan, however, has continued moving in new directions in recent years. Boosted by her ability at cowriting the script for *The Joy Luck Club*, she has been also collaborating on writing an opera based on her fourth novel, *The Bonesetter's Daughter*.

In the years to come, it is only certain that Amy Tan will continue to stretch her imagination and expand her flexibility as a writer. She will continue to produce writing that startles, inspires, and amazes her readers.

CHRONOLOGY

1924 Amy Tan's mother, Daisy Du Ching, is born in China.

1925 Tan's grandmother, Gu Jingmei, commits suicide to escape an unhappy second marriage.

1941 Daisy, herself struggling in an unhappy and abusive marriage, meets John Tan.

1945 Daisy and John meet again and begin a romance.

TIMELINE

1968
Amy's father, John, dies of a brain tumor.

1970
Amy meets Louis DeMattei.

1949
After two years in prison, Daisy travels to America to marry John Tan.

1924

1972

1924
Amy's mother, Daisy Du Ching, is born in China.

1952
An-Mei Ruth "Amy" Tan is born in Oakland, California.

1972
Tan graduates with her bachelor's degree.

1967
Amy's older brother, Peter Tan, dies of a brain tumor.

1947 Their relationship is discovered after Daisy attempts to run away with John, and Daisy is jailed for adultery. Heartbroken, John leaves for America.

1949 Daisy spends two years in prison and, on her release, travels to America to be with John, leaving behind her three young daughters.

1952 An-Mei Ruth "Amy" Tan is born in Oakland, California.

1960 Amy wins an essay contest sponsored by the local library about "What the Library Means to Me."

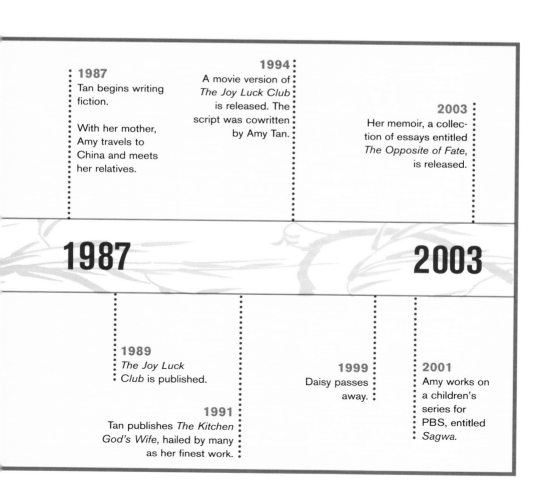

1987
Tan begins writing fiction.

With her mother, Amy travels to China and meets her relatives.

1994
A movie version of *The Joy Luck Club* is released. The script was cowritten by Amy Tan.

2003
Her memoir, a collection of essays entitled *The Opposite of Fate*, is released.

1987

2003

1989
The Joy Luck Club is published.

1991
Tan publishes *The Kitchen God's Wife*, hailed by many as her finest work.

1999
Daisy passes away.

2001
Amy works on a children's series for PBS, entitled *Sagwa*.

1967 Amy's older brother, Peter Tan, dies of a brain tumor.

1968 Amy's father, John, dies, also of a brain tumor. Soon after his death, Daisy takes Amy and her younger brother, John Jr., to live in Switzerland.

1969 Tan graduates with her high school degree and the family moves back to the United States. She enrolls in college, intent on studying medicine.

1970 Tan meets Louis DeMattei, a fellow student.

1972 Tan decides to drop out of the premed program and switches her focus to a double major in English and linguistics.

1972 Tan graduates with her bachelor's degree.

1973 Tan completes her master's degree. She begins a Ph.D. program in linguistics.

1976 Louis and Amy's good friend is murdered; his death shakes up Amy and forces her to reconsider her goals. She drops out of the doctoral program.

1978–1980 Using her knowledge of linguistics, Amy works with children who have speech impediments and learning disabilities.

1981 Frustrated with the way that she is marginalized as a minority, Amy begins a new career: freelance technical and corporate writing.

1987 Tired of the stress and lack of satisfaction that freelance writing brings her, Tan tries to write fiction. She enrolls in the Squaw Valley Community of Writers Workshop and writes a few successful short stories.

1987 With her mother, Amy travels to China and meets her relatives. Her agent, Sandy Dijkstra, negotiates a deal for a $50,000 advance for a book of short stories by Amy.

1988 Amy begins writing fiction full-time. She writes *The Joy Luck Club* within a few months.

1989 *The Joy Luck Club* is published and is an instant best seller.

1991 Tan publishes *The Kitchen God's Wife*, hailed by many as her finest work.

1992 With a friend as an illustrator, Tan publishes *The Moon Lady*, a children's book.

1992 With other fellow writers, such as Stephen King and Louise Erdrich, Amy joins the rock group, The Rock Bottom Remainders.

1994 A movie version of *The Joy Luck Club* is released; the script was cowritten by Amy Tan. Again with her friend, Amy publishes *The Chinese Siamese Cat*, a second children's book.

1995 Her third novel, *The Hundred Secret Senses*, is published and greeted with critical praise.

1999 Daisy, Amy's mother and greatest inspiration, passes away.

2001 After feeling ill for many months, Amy is diagnosed with Lyme disease. She is treated and returns to a normal working life.

2001 Her fourth book, *The Bonesetter's Daughter*, is released.

2001 Amy works on a children's series for PBS, entitled *Sagwa*.

2003 Her memoirs, a collection of essays entitled *The Opposite of Fate*, is released.

2005 *Saving Fish from Drowning*, her fifth novel, is released.

GLOSSARY

assimilate—To be absorbed into a different culture.

diaspora—A state in which many citizens of a nation are living outside its borders and, more often, abroad. Many talk about a Chinese diaspora that began in the 1900s and escalated after World War II, in which many Chinese emigrated to the United States.

genre—A literary category.

mah-jongg—An ancient pastime in which tiles are arranged symmetrically on a game board.

Orientalism—A racist view of Asian and Middle Eastern culture, in which the native peoples of these lands are portrayed as simple, uneducated, and often barbaric in comparison to people in Western lands.

patriarchy—A social system in which men dominate and women are relegated to an inferior status. Tan's novels usually portray the patriarchal society that existed in China before the Communist era.

polygamy—Marriage to more than one woman. Some marriages in pre-Communist China were polygamous; Tan writes about this issue in some of her fiction.

royalties—A payment to an author based on the number of books sold.

talk story—A device Amy Tan uses in her fiction, in which the women of the older, immigrant generation attempt to share their experiences with their American-born daughters.

BIBLIOGRAPHY

BOOKS

Huntley, E.D. *Amy Tan: A Critical Companion.* Critical Companions to Popular Contemporary Writers. Westport, Conn.: Greenwood Press, 1998.

Snodgrass, Mary Ellen. *Amy Tan: A Literary Companion.* Jefferson, N.C.: McFarland, 2004.

Tan, Amy. *The Opposite of Fate: Memoir of a Writing Life.* New York: Penguin Books, 2003.

———. *Saving Fish from Drowning.* New York: Putnam, 2005.

WEB SITES

"Amy Tan: Author Profile." Bookreporter.com. Available online. URL: http://www.bookreporter.com/authors/au-tan-amy.asp.

Jokinene, Anniina. "Biography." Anniina's Amy Tan Page. Available online. URL: http://www.luminarium.org/contemporary/amytan/. Updated on May 31, 2006.

King, Stephen. "Acceptance Speech." National Book Foundation. Available online. URL: http://www.nationalbook.org/nbaac-ceptspeech_sking.html.

Tan, Amy. Amytan.net. Available online. URL: http://www.amytan.net/.

FURTHER READING

BOOKS AND ARTICLES

"Amy Tan." *Current Biography* 53, no. 2 (February 1992): p. 55.

Chiu, Christina. *Notable Asian Americans: Literature and Education*. New York: Chelsea House, 1995.

Duke, Michael S., ed. *Modern Chinese Women Writers: Critical Appraisals*. New York: ME Sharpe, 1989.

Kim, Elaine. *Asian American Literature: An Introduction to the Writings and Their Social Context*. Philadelphia: Temple University Press, 1982.

Marvis, Barbara J. *Contemporary American Success Stories: Famous People of Asian Ancestry* vol. 4. Childs, Md.: Mitchell Lane, 1995.

Somogyi, Barbara, and David Stanton. *Poets and Writers Magazine* 19 (September–October 1991): p. 24.

Takaki, Robert. *Strangers from a Different Shore: A History of Asian Americans*. Boston: Little Brown, 1989.

WEB SITES

"Interview With Amy Tan." BBC Online. Available online. URL: http://www.bbc.co.uk/religion/programmes/belief/scripts/amy_tan.shtml.

"The Spirit Within: Interview With Amy Tan." *Salon Magazine Online*. Available online. URL: http://www.salon1999.com/12nov1995/feature/tan.html. February 29, 1997.

Tan, Amy. Amytan.net. Available online. URL: http://www.amytan.net/.

PHOTO CREDITS

INDEX

ABOUT THE AUTHOR

SUSAN MUADDI DARRAJ is an associate professor of English at Harford Community College in Bel Air, Maryland. She is also the editor of *The Baltimore Review*, a literary journal of fiction, poetry, and creative nonfiction. Her essays, articles, fiction, and reviews have appeared in *The Christian Science Monitor, New York Stories, Pages, The Greenwood Encyclopedia of Multi-Ethnic American Literature*, and elsewhere. Her short story collection, *The Inheritance of Exile*, is published by University of Notre Dame Press.